100 Reflections on Jesus: Imagining the Savior through Scripture

By Sean Patrick Shetler

*100 Reflections on Jesus:
Imagining the Savior through Scripture*

Copyright © 2025 Sean Patrick Shetler

Request for information should be submitted to Sean Patrick Shetler, 1829 Sleepy Holw., Kingsland, Texas 78639-5946

All rights reserved.

ISBN: 979-8-3104631-6-5

Cover and Interior Design: Sean Patrick Shetler

Printed in the United States of America

All Scripture quotations are from The ESV® Bible (The Holy Bible, English Standard Version ®), © 2001 by Crossway, a publishing ministry of Good News Publishers. Used by permission. All rights reserved. www.esv.org

All Scripture quotations marked (NLT) are taken from the *Holy Bible*, New Living Translation, copyright ©1996, 2004, 2015 by Tyndale House Foundation. Used by permission of Tyndale House Publishers, Carol Stream, Illinois 60188. All rights reserved.

All Scripture quotations taken from the Amplified Bible Copyright (AMP) © 2015 by The Lockman Foundation. Used by permission. All rights reserved.

THE GOOD SHEPHERD (JOHN 10:11-27)

DEDICATION

To my beloved wife, Libni "Libby" Shetler—the woman I have loved like no other. Your unwavering love, strength, and grace have been a constant light in my life. You are my greatest blessing, my dearest companion, helper, and you are the reflection of God's goodness and love in my journey.

This book is also dedicated to those who have come before me—faithful laborers who, by God's inspiration, have lain each brick of wisdom and truth to build His kingdom. As I now add my own, I do so in trust, knowing that others will also continue the work until the day of His glorious return.

To Him are all the glory, honor, and praise!

CONTENTS

	Infographic	iv
	Acknowledgements	1
1	Introduction	2
2	Jesus as Light and Lamp	14
3	Jesus as a Warrior	17
4	Jesus as Vine and Branches	20
5	Jesus as the Good Shepherd	23
6	Jesus as Refuge and Shield	26
7	Jesus as the Bread of Life	29
8	Jesus as the Living Water	32
9	Jesus as the Healer and Savior	36
10	Jesus as the Alpha and Omega	39
11	Jesus as the Victor and Eternal Hope	42
12	About the Author	45
13	Epilogue	52
14	Missions Application Project	90
	Bibliography	112

ACKNOWLEDGMENTS

First and foremost, I give thanks to **God Almighty**, the source of all wisdom, truth, and inspiration. Without His grace and guidance, this work would not be possible. May every word in these pages bring glory to His name and edify those who read them.

To my **beloved wife, Libni "Libby" Shetler**—your love, support, and unwavering faith have been a foundation of strength in my life. You have stood by me through every season, encouraging me with your wisdom and kindness. This journey would not be the same without you.

To my **family and friends**, who have lifted me up in prayer, offered encouragement, and provided invaluable insight along the way—thank you for believing in me and in the message of this book. Your love and support have been a gift beyond measure.

To the **mentors, teachers, and spiritual leaders** who have poured into my life—thank you for faithfully laying the bricks of wisdom and truth that have helped shape my understanding. Your dedication to the Kingdom has inspired me to continue building upon the foundation you have set.

To **every reader**—thank you for opening these pages and allowing these words to speak into your life. My prayer is that this book will strengthen your faith, challenge your heart, and draw you closer to God. May you be encouraged to take up the work and continue building His Kingdom, just as those before us have done.

To Him are all the glory, honor, and praise!

1 - INTRODUCTION

The purpose of *100 Reflections on Jesus* is to guide believers into a deeper, more intimate relationship with Christ through daily devotion and reflection. This book is designed to help cultivate spiritual formation by encouraging time in God's presence, meditating on His Word, and drawing closer to Jesus each day.

Each reflection serves as an opportunity to focus on who Jesus is—His character, His teachings, and His love for us—so that our hearts and minds may be transformed. As (**2 Corinthians 3:18**) reminds us, *"And we all, with unveiled face, beholding the glory of the Lord, are being transformed into the same image from one degree of glory to another."* Through these devotions, my hope is that readers will experience renewal, grow in faith, and be continually shaped into Christ's likeness. A key verse in my spiritual formation has been (**1 Thessalonians 5:21**), which instructs, *"But test everything; hold fast what is good."* This verse resonates with me because, throughout Church history, there have been many theologians with whom I disagree. However, even those I may not favor can offer valuable insights that contribute to the broader understanding of God's Kingdom.

One of my favorite verses penned by the Apostle Paul is (**2 Corinthians 3:2-3**): "You yourselves are our letter of recommendation, written on our hearts, to be known and read by all. And you show that you are a letter from Christ delivered by us, written not with ink but with the Spirit of the living God, not on tablets of stone but on tablets of human hearts." These verses emphasize that believers are living testimonies of Christ, with their transformed lives serving as proof of the gospel's power. Rather than being written on stone tablets like the Old Testament Law, this new covenant is inscribed on human hearts by the Spirit of the living God, demonstrating an internal, Spirit-led transformation.

It completely reshapes the meaning of the phrase "written in stone." Instead of rigid laws carved into tablets, God's truth is now inscribed on human hearts through the Holy Spirit. This transformation is not merely external but a living, dynamic work of God within us. Unlike the Old Testament Law written on stone tablets (**Exodus 31:18**), the new covenant is written on the hearts of believers through the Holy Spirit. Echoing this is (**Ezekiel

36:26) which highlights the internal transformation brought by the Sprit, replacing external legalism with a personal, living faith. Another key verse that has helped to shape me in my thinking and my spiritual formation is (**Philippians 1:27-28**): *"Only let your manner of life be worthy of the gospel of Christ, so that whether I come and see you or am absent, I may hear of you that you are standing firm in one spirit, with one mind striving side by side for the faith of the gospel, and not frightened in anything by your opponents. This is a clear sign to them of their destruction, but of your salvation, and that from God."*

This passage evokes the imagery of trench warfare in World War I, where soldiers stood shoulder to shoulder, unwavering in the face of relentless attacks. Just as they dug in, refusing to give ground, we as believers must stand firm in one spirit, holding the line against spiritual opposition. The phrase "striving side by side," reminds me of the camaraderie of troops advancing through the chaos of battle, relying on one another for strength, endurance, and survival. Faith is not fought in isolation—it is a collective effort, a shared struggle where we lock shields and push forward. Like soldiers emboldened by their cause, we must remain fearless, knowing that our perseverance is a sign of victory, secured not by our own strength but by the power of God.

Another set of critical verses that have profoundly shaped my spiritual formation are (**Colossians 1:15-18**), (**Philippians 2:5-11**) (the "Christ Hymn"), and (**Philippians 3:20-21**). Submission aligns with Christ's own example of obedience to the Father, as seen in (**Philippians 2:5-11**). Jesus, in His submission to the Father's will, exemplified perfect humility, even to the point of death on the cross (**Philippians 2:8**). When believers choose to place others' needs above their own, they reflect the self-giving love of God, embodying His kingdom values of unity, peace, and mutual care. In the fall of 2024, I felt the gentle yet unmistakable whisper of the Holy Spirit prompting me to take up and read (**Colossians 1:15-18**). The Spirit was drawing my attention to the powerful truth that Christ "holds all things together," is "the head of the Church," "the firstborn over all creation," and above everything is "preeminent." This revelation deepened my understanding of Christ's supreme authority and His sustaining presence in my life. It reminded me that no matter how chaotic life may seem; Jesus is sovereign, holding everything together by His divine power. These passages

1 - INTRODUCTION

continue to shape my faith, calling me to live in awe of Christ's majesty and to find my ultimate hope and identity in Him.

Humility, as a divine virtue, is not something we can manufacture on our own; it must be imparted to us through the indwelling of Christ in His divine humility. As Andrew Murray writes in *Humility: Essential Christian Classics*, "We have our pride from another, from Adam; we must have our humility from another too."[1]

A striking example of submission is found in Robert H. Schuller's *Tough Times Never Last, But Tough People Do!*[2] In a moment of deep uncertainty and feeling trapped, Schuller turned to prayer, seeking guidance. To his astonishment, the words that emerged were, "Tough times never last, but tough people do!" He credited this moment of clarity and inspiration to God, illustrating how submission to God's authority can bring wisdom, strength, and peace in the face of adversity.

Another key biblical foundation is seen in (**Mark 8:34-35**) where Jesus instructs His disciples, "If anyone would come after me, let him deny himself and take up his cross and follow me. For whoever would save his life will lose it, but whoever loses his life for my sake and the gospel's will save it." This passage emphasizes that submission involves self-denial and a willingness to sacrifice personal ambitions for the sake of Christ and His mission. True life is found in surrendering to God's purposes, reflecting a trust in His eternal plan.[3]

Furthermore, I find great encouragement in another passage— (**Hebrews 4:15-16**)—which reminds us: *"For we do not have a high priest who is unable to sympathize with our weaknesses, but one who in every respect has been tempted as we are, yet without sin. Let us then with confidence draw near to the throne of grace, that we may receive mercy and find grace to help in time of need."*

---

[1] Andrew Murray, *Humility: Essential Christian Classics* (CreateSpace Independent Publishing Platform, November 2, 2014), 17-18.

[2] Robert H. Schuller, *Tough Times Never Last, But Tough People Do!* (Nashville, TN: Thomas Nelson, 1983), 29-30.

[3] Richard J. Foster, *Celebration of Discipline: The Path to Spiritual Growth*, Special Anniversary Edition (San Francisco: HarperOne, 2018), 114-115.

1 - INTRODUCTION

Moreover, meditation is another spiritual discipline I have been focusing on recently. It involves continually reflecting on a word, phrase, or insight revealed by the Spirit. The Greek word *meletaō* (μελετάω, Strong's #3191), used in (**1 Timothy 4:13-15**), conveys the idea of deep contemplation—painstakingly considering a matter. This practice is a time of pondering and internalizing the message. I like to think of it as "chewing on the fat" or "chewing on spiritual bubble gum." Similarly, the Hebrew word *hagah* (הָגָה, Strong's #1897) is often translated as "meditate," "mutter," or "speak." It emphasizes thoughtful reflection, particularly in the context of Scripture, as seen in passages like (**Joshua 1:8**) and (**Psalm 1:2**).[4]

This journey has solidified my belief that, through Him, I can face life's trials, tribulations, and temptations with hope, grace, and resilience, knowing that His presence sustains me every step of the way. As (**Jeremiah 17:7-8**) says, "Blessed is the one who trusts in the Lord, whose confidence is in Him. They will be like a tree planted by the water that sends out its roots by the stream. It does not fear when heat comes; its leaves are always green. It has no worries in a year of drought and never fails to bear fruit." Similarly, (**Psalm 1:2-3**) encourages, "But whose delight is in the law of the Lord, and who meditates on His law day and night. That person is like a tree planted by streams of water, which yields its fruit in season and whose leaf does not wither—whatever they do prospers." These verses remind me to remain rooted in God's Word, trusting that, no matter the circumstances, His strength will carry me through.

Whether you seek encouragement, wisdom, or a deeper understanding of Jesus, may these reflections be a daily invitation to walk with Him, dwell in His presence, and be transformed by His grace. May they draw you closer to His heart, strengthening your faith and be renewed by the Spirit each day.

Also, another set of verses that has helped me focus on spiritual growth is (**Colossians 3:1-5**):

"If then you have been raised with Christ, seek the things that are above, where Christ is, seated at the right hand of God. Set your minds on things that are above, not on things that are on earth. For you have died, and your life is hidden with Christ in God. When

---

[4] William D. Mounce, *Mounce's Complete Expository Dictionary of Old & New Testament Words* (Grand Rapids, MI: Zondervan, 2006), 922–1208.

Christ who is your life appears, then you also will appear with him in glory. Put to death therefore what is earthly in you: sexual immorality, impurity, passion, evil desire, and covetousness, which is idolatry."

This passage calls believers to a heavenly mindset, reminding us that our true identity is in Christ. Since we have been spiritually raised with Him, our focus should not be on the temporary things of this world but on eternal realities. Paul urges us to let go of sinful desires and instead live in the righteousness and holiness that reflect our new life in Christ. It is a call to transformation, aligning our hearts and actions with God's will as we anticipate the glory of His coming.

Lastly, a verse that has deeply resonated with me, yet is often overlooked, especially in ministry, is (**Ephesians 4:11-12**): "And he gave the apostles, the prophets, the evangelists, the shepherds and teachers, to equip the saints for the work of ministry, for building up the body of Christ."

Battle Rhythm: Praying the Lord's Model Prayer

On the night of Wednesday, November 13, 2024, I found myself unable to sleep, deeply meditating on (Matthew 6:9-13), the Lord's Prayer. Despite my attempts to rest, the words of this prayer echoed in my mind, compelling me to explore ways to internalize its profound meaning. This led me to experiment with acronyms and mnemonic devices to better grasp the structure and significance of the Lord's Prayer.

In my CHRI-6314 (Missions and Evangelism) class, we were studying Chapter 16 of *Missions: Biblical Foundations and Contemporary Strategies* by Dr. Gailyn Van Rheenen. On page 394-395, the book presents a prayer framework developed by Mike Breen and Steve Cockram (2009), which organizes the Lord's Prayer into six segments.[5] However, as I reflected on their model, I began to see ways it could be refined and expanded. I started conceptualizing a new approach, which I've titled "The Lord's Model Prayer" aka "CHRIST'S Framework." The CHRIST'S acronym holds a layered significance: it not only spells "CHRIST'S," emphasizing Christ's

---

[5] Gailyn Van Rheenan, *Missions: Biblical Foundations and Contemporary Strategies* (Grand Rapids: Zondervan, 2014), 394-395.

1 - INTRODUCTION

possession of the prayer, but it also expands the framework to include seven facets instead of six.

This adjustment transforms the model into a heptagon (seven sides) versus a hexagon (six sides) in the older model. The CHRIST's model or framework was created to align with the biblical symbolism of completeness and perfection seen in the seven days of creation. By aligning the prayer's structure with this divine number, the CHRIST'S Framework or model underscores the theological richness and completeness of the Lord's Model Prayer.

The Lord's Model Prayer: CHRIST's Framework (7 Parts)

A. Old Framework vs. New Framework

Prayer serves as the bedrock of the Christian faith, underpinning all spiritual disciplines and practices. This proposal does not claim to introduce a new concept but seeks to offer a renewed perspective on an existing framework developed by previous scholars. I have titled this refreshed model the CHRIST'S Framework, which expands the traditional structure of the Lord's Prayer into seven distinct parts.

In Chapter 16 of Dr. Gailyn Van Rheenen's *Missions: Biblical Foundations and Contemporary Strategies*, he emphasizes the profound impact of the Lord's Prayer under "Rhythm 6: Praying the Model Prayer": "Praying through the Lord's Prayer places God in control of our lives. The prayer nurtures dependence, leads to confession, shapes identity, and comforts our souls. It is the most touching and transforming spiritual discipline that we do" (*Missions*, 394-395).[6] The widely used model by Mike Breen and Steve Cockram (2009), revisited in Van Rheenen's text, categorizes the Lord's Prayer into six elements (CKPFGP): The Father's Character (*Matt. 6:9*), Kingdom (*Matt. 6:10*), Provision (*Matt. 6:11*), Forgiveness (*Matt. 6:12*), Guidance (*Matt. 6:13a*), and Protection (*Matt. 6:13b*). This framework, depicted as a hexagon in Figure 16.9 on page 394 of the textbook, provides a structured and practical approach to prayer (*Building a Discipling Culture*, 155-167).[7]

---

[6] Gailyn Van Rheenan, *Missions: Biblical Foundations and Contemporary Strategies* (Grand Rapids: Zondervan, 2014), 394-395.

[7] See Michael D. Coogan, ed., *The Annotated Oxford Bible: New Revised Standard Version*. 5th ed. (New York: Oxford University Press, 2018), 1790-1791 (Matt. 6:9-13); Mike Breen and Steve Cockram, *Building a Discipling Culture* (Pauley's Island,

However, through deeper meditation, I realized that the six-part model feels incomplete when weighed against biblical themes of divine perfection and wholeness. In Scripture, the number seven symbolizes completion and fullness, as seen in the seven days of creation. If Jesus's prayer was meant as the ultimate model, it is reasonable to propose that it should reflect this pattern of divine completeness. Therefore, I offer an expanded framework—the CHRIST'S Framework—which incorporates a seventh element, aligning the prayer with the biblical number of perfection, divinity, and completeness.

The CHRIST'S acronym is purposefully crafted to highlight both Christ's ownership and the framework's comprehensive nature. Spelling out "CHRIST'S" underscores that this prayer is rooted in and reflective of Christ's teachings. It enhances the traditional model by offering deeper insight into the spiritual and theological dimensions of the prayer, while simultaneously presenting a practical, seven-sided framework for daily devotion. This framework carries multiple layers of meaning, enriching its significance.

B. The Lord's Model Prayer: CHRIST'S Framework (7 Parts)

1. **C – Call (Mt. 6:11, The Father's Provision):**
   "Give us this day our daily bread."
   Call represents earnestly asking God for provision. This involves making our needs known to Him, trusting that He provides for us daily.
2. **H – Honor (Mt. 6:9a, The Father's Character):**
   "Our Father in heaven, hallowed be your name."
   Honor refers to revering God's name through praise, worship, and acknowledging His holiness. It focuses on glorifying God's character.[8]
3. **R – Repentance (Mt. 6:12, The Father's Forgiveness):**
   "Forgive us our debts, as we also have forgiven our debtors."
   Repentance emphasizes seeking God's forgiveness for our sins

---

SC: 3DM, 2009; revised 2011), 155-167.

[8] Tim Keller. "Basis of Prayer: 'Our Father,'" Sermon, April 23, 1995, http://sermons2.redeemer.com/sermons/basis-prayer-our-father (accessed November 13, 2024).

1 - INTRODUCTION

and extending forgiveness to others, reflecting our need for God's mercy.

4. **I – Intercession (Mt. 6:10, The Father's Kingdom):**
   "Your kingdom come, your will be done on earth as it is in heaven."
   Intercession involves praying for God's kingdom to manifest on earth and for His will to prevail in all things. This step focuses on aligning with God's purposes.[9]
5. **S – Surrender (Mt. 6:9b, The Father's Authority):**
   "Your kingdom come."
   Surrender is the act of yielding our lives to God's sovereign will, recognizing His authority over every aspect of our lives.
6. **T – Temptation (Mt. 6:13a, The Father's Guidance and Protection):**
   "And lead us not into temptation."
   Temptation focuses on asking for God's guidance and strength to resist the allure of sin. We rely on Him to lead us away from paths that could harm our spiritual walk.
7. **S – Salvation (Mt. 6:13b, The Father's Deliverance):**
   "But deliver us from the evil one."
   Salvation refers to praying for deliverance from the evil one, seeking God's protection and redemption. This encompasses both spiritual and physical salvation from harm.

The Lord's Model Prayer: CHRIST'S Framework (7 Parts)

The CHRIST'S Framework is intentionally designed to reflect the shape of a heptagon, a seven-sided figure, symbolizing completeness and perfection in a biblical sense. Just as the heptagon is geometrically balanced and interconnected, the seven parts of this framework form a cohesive, harmonious guide for spiritual growth and daily devotion.

Symbol of Completeness and Perfection
(7 Signifies Divine Perfection)

In Scripture, the number seven often signifies divine perfection and wholeness. For example: The seven days of creation culminate in God's rest, symbolizing completion (Genesis 2:2-3). The sevenfold Spirit of God in Revelation reflects the fullness of His presence (Revelation 1:4). The heptagonal shape, therefore, is a fitting

---

[9] Mark Hamilton, ed., *Transforming Word: One-Volume Commentary on the Bible* (Abilene, TX: Abilene Christian University Press, 2009), 739.

metaphor for the CHRIST'S Framework, which aims to encompass the fullness of Christian prayer and spiritual practice.

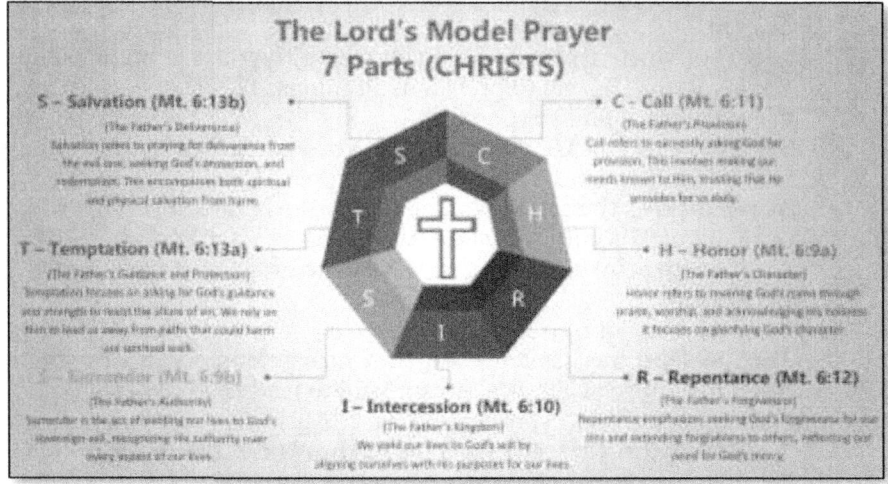

Mnemonic Device and Structural Insights:

The **CHRIST'S** acronym and mnemonic device not only captures the essence of the Lord's Prayer but also centers it on Christ (Christology), emphasizing how each element aligns with His teachings and mission.

Pairs (2 Pairs):

Honor and **Surrender** (H & S): focus on revering God and submitting to His will.

Temptation and **Salvation** (T & S): highlight protection and deliverance.

1 - INTRODUCTION

Triplet (Triad):

The middle elements—**Call**, **Repentance**, and **Intercession**—focus on our relational, spiritual, and communal needs. This structure brings the elements of the Lord's Prayer into a Christ-centered focus (*Christology*), making it easier to internalize and apply in personal devotion.[10]

Three Meanings in the CHRIST's Framework

The Lord's Model Prayer, often called the "Lord's Prayer" and the CHRIST'S Framework are rich with layers of meaning that can be explored through a "triplet"[11] or three-fold understanding.

Here is how the CHRIST's Framework reflects at least three meanings:

I. Theological Meaning: A Reflection of Christ's Ownership

A. Covenantal Relationship:

The acronym emphasizes that the prayer originates from Christ and is rooted in His covenant with His followers. It highlights Christ's role as teacher and mediator, demonstrating His divine authority.

B. Complete Submission:

Each element of the framework reinforces submission to God's will, mirroring Christ's submission to the Father as seen in the prayer, "Your will be done on earth as it is in heaven" (Matt. 6:10).

---

[10] Hillerbrand, H. J. and Stefon, . Matt. "Christology." Encyclopedia Britannica, July 30, 2022. https://www.britannica.com/topic/Christology.

[11] Merriam-Webster.com Dictionary, s.v. "triplet," accessed December 9, 2024, https://www.merriam-webster.com/dictionary/triplet.

1 - INTRODUCTION

C. Perfection in Seven:

The number seven symbolizes perfection or completeness in biblical tradition. The CHRIST'S acronym reflects Christ's perfect teaching and the completeness of the prayer model.

II. Devotional Meaning: A Seven-Sided Daily Framework

A. Holistic Spiritual Growth:

Each letter in "CHRIST'S" can correspond to aspects of devotion (e.g., **C** for **Call**, **H** for **Honor**, etc.), encouraging believers to cultivate a balanced spiritual life.

B. Comprehensive Prayer Guide:

The seven-sided structure serves as a practical tool for deepening daily prayer life, ensuring it is comprehensive, encompassing adoration, confession, thanksgiving, intercession, and supplication.

C. Accessible Depth:

While simple enough for daily use, the framework invites deeper reflection, making it adaptable for both new believers and mature Christians.

III. Spiritual Meaning: A Triple Reflection of God's Nature

A. Trinitarian Insight: The framework subtly reflects the Trinity (**Matthew 28:19**), with three primary levels of meaning aligning with the Father (source of provision and protection), the Son (teaching and intercession), and the Spirit (guidance and sanctification).

B. Christocentric Focus:

The model emphasizes that prayer is through Christ, to the Father, by the Spirit, reflecting (John 14:6), "I am the way, and the truth, and the life. No one comes to the Father except through me."

1 - INTRODUCTION

C. Symbolic Perfection:

The seven parts can mirror the seven days of creation, God's covenant completeness, and the perfection of divine will, emphasizing spiritual wholeness.

D. Concluding Thought

The **CHRIST'S Framework** serves as both a practical tool for daily prayer and a rich expression of theological, devotional, and spiritual truths. Each layer of understanding intertwines to deepen the believer's relationship with God, ensuring that this prayer remains timeless, transformative, and profoundly effective for spiritual formation.

Three Thoughts on The Holy Spirit

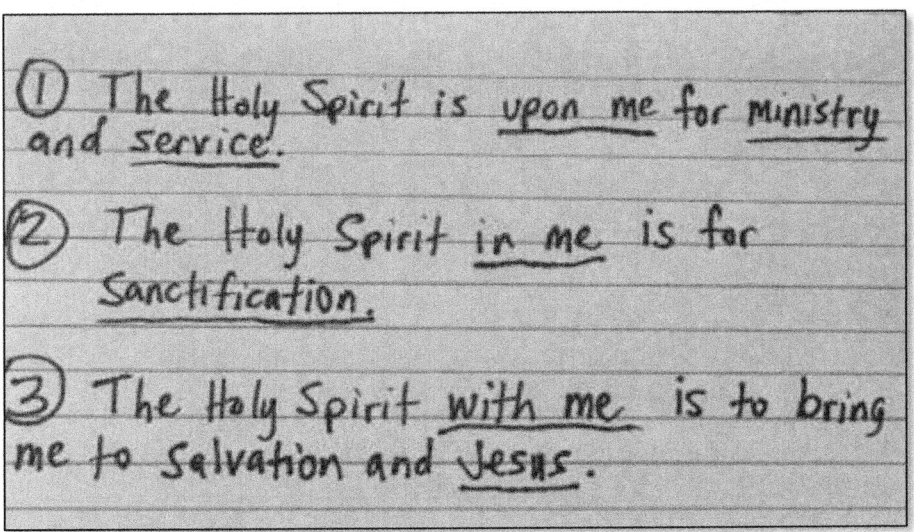

① The Holy Spirit is upon me for ministry and service.

② The Holy Spirit in me is for Sanctification.

③ The Holy Spirit with me is to bring me to Salvation and Jesus.

2 – JESUS AS LIGHT AND LAMP

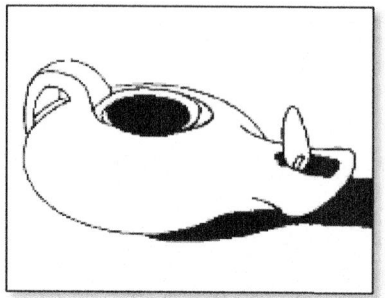

1. Jesus is the lamp.

Psalm 119:105: "Your word is a lamp to my feet and a light to my path."

2. Jesus is the light.

John 1:5: "The light shines in the darkness, and the darkness has not overcome it."

3. Jesus is the light of the world.

John 8:12: "Again Jesus spoke to them, saying, 'I am the light of the world. Whoever follows me will not walk in darkness, but will have the light of life.'"

4. Jesus is the sun of righteousness, rising with healing in His wings.

Malachi 4:2: "But for you who fear my name, the sun of righteousness shall rise with healing in its wings. You shall go out leaping like calves from the stall."

5. Jesus is the bright morning star, guiding me in the night.

Revelation 22:16: "I, Jesus, have sent my angel to testify to you about these things for the churches. I am the root and the descendant of David, the bright morning star."

6. Jesus has come into the world as light.

John 12:46: "I have come into the world as light, so that whoever believes in me may not remain in darkness."

2 – JESUS AS LIGHT AND LAMP

7. Jesus is the great light.

Isaiah 9:2: "The people who walked in darkness have seen a great light; those who dwelt in a land of deep darkness, on them has light shone."

8. Jesus reflects His light through us.

Matthew 5:14-16: "You are the light of the world. A city set on a hill cannot be hidden. Nor do people light a lamp and put it under a basket, but on a stand, and it gives light to all in the house. In the same way, let your light shine before others, so that they may see your good works and give glory to your Father who is in heaven."

9. Jesus now shines spiritual light into our hearts.

2 Corinthians 4:6: "For God, who said, 'Let light shine out of darkness,' has shone in our hearts to give the light of the knowledge of the glory of God in the face of Jesus Christ."

10. Jesus is the light which means living in truth, righteousness, and fellowship with God.

1 John 1:5-7: "This is the message we have heard from him and proclaim to you, that God is light, and in him is no darkness at all. If we say we have fellowship with him while we walk in darkness, we lie and do not practice the truth. But if we walk in the light, as he is in the light, we have fellowship with one another, and the blood of Jesus his Son cleanses us from all sin."

2 – JESUS AS LIGHT AND LAMP

In Summary:

1. **Jesus is the lamp**, illuminating the path of righteousness and guiding our steps through the darkness (Psalm 119:105).

2. **Jesus is the light,** shining in the midst of darkness, and no power of evil can overcome Him (John 1:5).

3. **Jesus is the light of the world**, offering salvation to all who follow Him, leading them out of darkness and into eternal life (John 8:12).

4. **Jesus is the sun of righteousness**, rising with healing in His wings, bringing restoration and joy to those who fear His name (Malachi 4:2).

5. **Jesus is the bright morning star**, a guiding light in the night, leading His people with truth and unwavering hope (Revelation 22:16).

6. **Jesus has come into the world as light**, so that all who believe in Him will no longer remain in darkness but will walk in His truth (John 12:46).

7. **Jesus is the great light**, shining upon those who once walked in deep darkness, bringing life, redemption, and the glory of God (Isaiah 9:2).

8. **Jesus reflects His light through us**, calling us to shine brightly in a dark world so that others may see His truth and give glory to God (Matthew 5:14-16).

9. **Jesus now shines spiritual light into our hearts**, revealing the glory of God and transforming us with His divine wisdom (2 Corinthians 4:6).

10. **Jesus is the light, and to walk in His light is to live in truth, righteousness, and fellowship** with God and one another (1 John 1:5-7).

3 - JESUS AS A WARRIOR

11. Jesus is the commander of heaven's armies.

Joshua 5:14: "And he said, 'No; but I am the commander of the army of the Lord. Now I have come.' And Joshua fell on his face to the earth and worshiped and said to him, 'What does my Lord say to his servant?'"

12. Jesus is the mighty man of war.

Exodus 15:3: "The Lord is a man of war; the Lord is His name."

13. Jesus is the armor of God.

Ephesians 6:11: "Put on the whole armor of God that you may be able to stand against the schemes of the devil."

14. Jesus is the conquering king.

Revelation 19:11: "Then I saw heaven opened, and behold, a white horse! The one sitting on it is called Faithful and True, and in righteousness he judges and makes war."

15. Jesus is the sword of truth.

Hebrews 4:12: "For the word of God is living and active, sharper than any two-edged sword, piercing to the division of soul and of spirit, of joints and of marrow, and discerning the thoughts and intentions of the heart."

16. Jesus is the victorious champion.

Colossians 2:15: "He disarmed the rulers and authorities and put them to open shame, by triumphing over them in Him."

3 - JESUS AS A WARRIOR

17. Jesus is the ruler who strikes down nations.

Revelation 19:15: "From His mouth comes a sharp sword with which to strike down the nations, and He will rule them with a rod of iron. He will read the winepress of the fury of the wrath of God the Almighty."

18. Jesus is the warrior who crushes Satan underfoot.

Genesis 3:15: "I will put enmity between you and the woman, and between your offspring and her offspring; he shall bruise your head, and you shall bruise his heel."

19. Jesus is the armed champion who rides in majesty.

Psalm 45:3-4: "Gird your sword on your thigh, O mighty one, in your splendor and majesty! In your majesty ride out victoriously for the cause of truth and meekness and righteousness; let your right hand teach your awesome deeds!"

20. Jesus is the battle cry that rallies his people.

Isaiah 42:13: "The Lord goes out like a might man, like a man of war he stirs up his zeal; He cries out, He shouts aloud, He shows himself mighty against his foes."

3 - JESUS AS A WARRIOR

In Summary:

11. **Jesus is the Commander of Heaven's Armies**, leading the forces of righteousness and fighting on behalf of His people (Joshua 5:14).

12. **Jesus is the Mighty Man of War**, standing victorious over all evil, never defeated in battle (Exodus 15:3).

13. **Jesus is the Armor of God**, equipping believers with divine strength to stand against the enemy (Ephesians 6:11).

14. **Jesus is the Conquering King,** riding in triumph to establish justice and truth (Revelation 19:11).

15. **Jesus is the Sword of Truth,** piercing through lies and exposing the thoughts and intentions of every heart (Hebrews 4:12).

16. **Jesus is the Victorious Champion,** disarming the powers of darkness and putting them to open shame (Colossians 2:15).

17. **Jesus is the Ruler Who Strikes Down Nations,** executing judgment and reigning with a rod of iron (Revelation 19:15).

18. **Jesus is the Warrior Who Crushes Satan Underfoot,** fulfilling God's promise of ultimate victory over evil (Genesis 3:15).

19. **Jesus is the Armed Champion Who Rides in Majesty,** advancing in righteousness, truth, and meekness (Psalm 45:3-4).

20. **Jesus is the Battle Cry That Rallies His People,** stirring up zeal and calling His followers to stand firm in faith (Isaiah 42:13).

4 - JESUS AS THE VINE AND THE BRANCHES

21. Jesus is the vine that connects me to the Father.

John 15:1: "I am the true vine, and my Father is the vinedresser."

22. Jesus is the fruitful branch who brings righteousness.

Jeremiah 23:5: "Behold, the days are coming, declares the Lord, when I will raise up for David a righteous branch, and he shall reign as king and deal wisely, and shall execute justice and righteousness in the land."

23. Jesus is the tree of life, offering eternal sustenance.

Revelation 22:2: "Through the middle of the street of the city; also on either side of the river, the tree of life with its twelve kinds of fruit, yielding its fruit each month. The leaves of the tree were for the healing of the nations."

24. Jesus is the vine that unites all believers as one body.

Romans 12:5: "So we, though many, are one body in Christ, and individually members one of another."

25. Jesus is the root of Jesse, from whom all life springs.

Isaiah 11:1: "There shall come forth a shoot from the stump of Jesse, and a branch from his roots shall bear fruit."

4 - JESUS AS THE VINE AND THE BRANCHES

26. Jesus is the vine that bears the fruit of the Spirit in us.

Galatians 5:22-23: "But the fruit of the Spirit is love, joy, peace, patience, kindness, goodness, faithfulness, gentleness, self-control; against such things there is no law."

27. Jesus is the vine that produces good fruit, not bad.

Matthew 7:17-18: "So, every healthy tree bears good fruit, but the diseased tree bears bad fruit. A healthy tree cannot bear bad fruit, nor can a diseased tree bear good fruit."

28. Jesus is the vine that restores what was broken.

Joel 2:25: "I will restore to you the years that the swarming locust has eaten, the hopper, the destroyer, and the cutter, my great army, which I sent among you."

29. Jesus is the branch that covers us in His grace.

Isaiah 4:2: "In that day the branch of the Lord shall be beautiful and glorious, and the fruit of the land shall be the pride and honor of the survivors of Israel."

30. Jesus is the vine, and we are the branches.

John 15:5: "I am the vine; you are the branches. Whoever abides in me and I in him, he it is that bears much fruit, for apart from me you can do nothing."

4 - JESUS AS THE VINE AND THE BRANCHES

In Summary:

21. Jesus is the vine that connects me to the Father.
Jesus is the true vine, and through Him, we are connected to God, the vinedresser who nurtures and cares for us (John 15:1).

22. Jesus is the fruitful branch who brings righteousness.
As the righteous branch from David's line, Jesus reigns with wisdom, justice, and righteousness (Jeremiah 23:5).

23. Jesus is the tree of life, offering eternal sustenance.
Just as the tree of life bears fruit for healing, Jesus provides eternal nourishment and restoration (Revelation 22:2).

24. Jesus is the vine that unites all believers as one body.
In Christ, we are many members but one body, connected through His love and purpose (Romans 12:5).

25. Jesus is the root of Jesse, from whom all life springs.
Jesus is the prophesied shoot from Jesse's lineage, the source of spiritual life and fruitfulness (Isaiah 11:1).

26. Jesus is the vine that bears the fruit of the Spirit in us.
Through our connection to Christ, we produce the fruits of love, joy, peace, and righteousness (Galatians 5:22-23).

27. Jesus is the vine that produces good fruit, not bad.
A healthy vine bears good fruit, and through Christ, our lives reflect His goodness and truth (Matthew 7:17-18).

28. Jesus is the vine that restores what was broken.
He renews and restores what was lost, bringing healing and redemption (Joel 2:25).

29. Jesus is the branch that covers us in His grace.
He is the beautiful and glorious branch of the Lord, offering His grace and protection (Isaiah 4:2).

30. Jesus is the vine, and we are the branches.
Our very existence and spiritual growth depend on abiding in Him, for apart from Him, we can do nothing (John 15:5).

5 - JESUS AS THE GOOD SHEPHERD

31. Jesus is the Good Shepherd Who Lays Down His Life.

John 10:11: "I am the good shepherd. The good shepherd lays down his life for the sheep."

32. Jesus is the Shepherd Who Knows His Sheep.

John 10:14-15: "I am the good shepherd. I know my own and my own know me, just as the Father knows me and I know the Father; and I lay down my life for the sheep."

33. Jesus is the Shepherd Who Leaves the 99 for the 1.

Luke: 15:4-5: "What man of you, having a hundred sheep, if he has lost one of them, does not leave the ninety-nine in the open country, and go after the one that is lost, until he finds it?"

34. Jesus is the Shepherd who is Gathering His Flock.

Isaiah 40:11: "He will tend his flock like a shepherd; he will gather the lambs in his arms; he will carry them in his bosom, and gently lead those that are with young."

35. Jesus says, My Sheep Hear My Voice.

John 10:27: "My sheep hear my voice, and I know them, and they follow me."

36. Jesus is the Shepherd Who Goes Seeking the Lost Sheep.

Ezekiel 34:11-12: "For thus says the Lord God: Behold, I, myself will search for my sheep and will seek them out. As a shepherd seeks out his flock when he is among his sheep that have been scattered, so will I seek out my sheep…"

37. Jesus is the Shepherd Who Calls By Name.

John 10:3-4: "The sheep hear his voice, and he calls his own sheep by name and leads them out. When he has brought out all his own, he goes before them, and the sheep follow him, for they know his voice."

38. Jesus is the Shepherd Who Restores the Soul.

Psalm 23:3: "He restores my soul. He leads me in paths of righteousness for his name's sake."

39. Jesus is the Shepherd who appoints Overseers.

1 Peter 5:2-4: "Shepherd the flock of God that is among young, exercising oversight, not under compulsion, but willingly, as God would have you; not for shameful gain, but eagerly...And when the chief Shepherd appears, you will receive the unfading crown of glory."

40. Jesus is the Shepherd who anoints.

Psalm 23:5-6: "You prepare a table before me in the presence of my enemies; you anoint my head with oil; my cup overflows. Surely goodness and mercy shall follow me all the days of my life, and I shall dwell in the house of the Lord forever."

5 - JESUS AS THE GOOD SHEPHERD

In Summary:

31. **Jesus is the Good Shepherd Who Lays Down His Life** (John 10:11).

32. **Jesus is the Shepherd Who Knows His Sheep** (John 10:14-15).

33. **Jesus is the Shepherd Who Leaves the 99** (Luke 15:4-5).

34. **Jesus is the Shepherd Who is Gathering His Flock** (Isaiah 40:11).

35. **Jesus Says, My Sheep Hear My Voice** (John 10:27).

36. **Jesus is the Shepherd Who Goes Seeking the Lost Sheep** (Ezekiel 34:11-12).

37. **Jesus is the Shepherd Who Calls by Name** (John 10:3-4).

38. **Jesus is the Shepherd Who Restores the Soul** (Psalm 23:3).

39. **Jesus is the Shepherd Who Appoints Overseers** (1 Peter 5:2-4).

40. **Jesus is the Shepherd Who Anoints** (Psalm 23:5-6).

6 - JESUS AS REFUGE AND SHIELD

41. Jesus is a refuge and a very present help in trouble.

Psalm 46:1-2: "God is our refuge and strength, a very present help in trouble. Therefore we will not fear though the earth gives way, though the mountains be moved into the heart of the sea."

42. Jesus is a strong fortress.

Psalm 18:2: "The Lord is my rock and my fortress and my deliverer, my God, my rock, in whom I take refuge, my shield, and the horn of my salvation, my stronghold."

43. Jesus is a shadow of protection.

Psalm 91:1: "He who dwells in the shelter of the Most High will abide in the shadow of the Almighty."

44. Jesus is a high tower.

Proverbs 18:10: "The name of the Lord is a strong tower; the righteous man runs into it and is safe."

45. Jesus is a stronghold for the oppressed.

Psalm 9:9: "The Lord is a stronghold for the oppressed, a stronghold in times of trouble."

6 - JESUS AS REFUGE AND SHIELD

46. Jesus is a shield of protection.

Psalm 3:3: "But you, O Lord, are a shield about me, my glory, and the lifter of my head."

47. Jesus is a shield for the righteous.

Proverbs 30:5: "Every word of God proves true; he is a shield to those who take refuge in him."

48. Jesus is our shield in battle.

Psalm 18:30: "This God—his way is perfect; the word of the Lord proves true; he is a shield for all those who take refuge in him."

49. Jesus is our shield which can extinguish all the flaming darts.

Ephesians 6:16: "In all circumstances take up the shield of faith, with which you can extinguish all the flaming darts of the evil one."

50. Jesus is a our defender against fear.

Genesis 15:1: "After these things the word of the Lord came to Abram in a vision: 'Fear not, Abram, I am your shield; your reward shall be very great."

In Summary:

41. **Jesus is a refuge and a very present help in trouble** (Psalm 46:1-2).

42. **Jesus is a strong fortress** (Psalm 18:2).

43. **Jesus is a shadow of protection** (Psalm 91:1).

44. **Jesus is a high tower** (Proverbs 18:10).

45. **Jesus is a stronghold for the oppressed** (Psalm 9:9).

46. **Jesus is a shield of protection** (Psalm 3:3).

47. **Jesus is a shield for the righteous** (Proverbs 30:5).

48. **Jesus is our shield in battle** (Psalm 18:30).

49. **Jesus is our shield which can extinguish all the flaming darts** (Ephesians 6:16).

50. **Jesus is our defender against fear** (Genesis 15:1).

7 - JESUS AS THE BREAD OF LIFE

51. Jesus, the Bread that Sustains the Soul.

Matthew 4:4: "But he answered, 'It is written, "Man shall not live by bread alone, but by every word that comes from the mouth of God."

52. Jesus is the True Bread from Heaven.

John 6:32-33: "Jesus then said to them, 'Truly, truly, I say to you, it was not Moses who gave you the bread from heaven, but my Father gives you the true bread from heaven. For the bread of God is he who comes down from heaven and gives life to the world.'"

53. Jesus is the Bread of Life.

John 6:35: "Jesus said to them, 'I am the bread of life; whoever comes to me shall not hunger, and whoever believes in me shall never thirst.'"

54. Jesus is the Bread that Satisfies the Hungry.

Matthew 5:6: "Blessed are those who hunger and thirst for righteousness, for they shall be satisfied."

55. Jesus is the Bread Broken for Us.

Luke 22:19: "And he took bread, and when he had given thanks, he broke it and gave it to them, saying, 'This is my body, which is given for you. Do this in remembrance of me.'"

56. Jesus is the Bread of Unity.

1 Corinthians 10:17: "Because there is one bread, we who are many are one body, for we all partake of the one bread."

7 - JESUS AS THE BREAD OF LIFE

57. Jesus is the Daily Bread that Sustains.

Matthew 6:11: "Give us this day our daily bread."

58. Jesus is the Bread that Never Perishes.

John 6:27: "Do not work for the food that perishes, but for the food that endures to eternal life, which the Son of Man will give to you."

59. Jesus is the Living Bread.

John 6:51: "I am the living bread that came down from heaven. If anyone eats of this bread, he will live forever. And the bread that I will give for the life of the world is my flesh."

60. Jesus is the Bread that Multiplies.

Matthew 14:19-20: "Then he ordered the crowds to sit down on the grass, and taking the five loaves and the two fish, he looked up to heaven and said a blessing. Then he broke the loaves and gave them to the disciples, and the disciples gave them to the crowds. And they all ate and were satisfied."

7 - JESUS AS THE BREAD OF LIFE

In Summary:

51. **Jesus, the Bread that Sustains the Soul** (Matthew 4:4).

52. **Jesus is the True Bread from Heaven** (John 6:32-33).

53. **Jesus is the Bread of Life** (John 6:35).

54. **Jesus is the Bread that Satisfies the Hungry** (Matthew 5:6).

55. **Jesus is the Bread Broken for Us** (Luke 22:19).

56. **Jesus is the Bread of Unity** (1 Corinthians 10:17).

57. **Jesus is the Daily Bread that Sustains** (Matthew 6:11).

58. **Jesus is the Bread that Never Perishes** (John 6:27).

59. **Jesus is the Living Bread** (John 6:51).

60. **Jesus is the Bread that Multiplies** (Matthew 14:19-20).

8 – JESUS AS THE LIVING WATER

61. Jesus is the wellspring of life, refreshing my soul.

John 7:37-38: "On the last day of the feast, the great day, Jesus stood up and cried out, 'If anyone thirsts, let him come to me and drink. Whoever believes in me, as the Scripture has said, 'Out of his heart will flow rivers of living water.'"

62. Jesus is the fountain of living water, quenching my thirst forever.

Jeremiah 2:13: "For my people have committed two evils: they have forsaken me, the fountain of living waters, and hewed out cisterns for themselves, broken cisterns that can hold no water."

63. Jesus is the water that makes the desert bloom.

Isaiah 35:6-7: "Then shall the lame man leap like a deer, and the tongue of the mute sing for joy. For waters break forth in the wilderness, and streams in the desert; the burning sand shall become a pool, and the thirsty ground springs of water; in the haunt of jackals, where they lie down, the grass shall become reeds and rushes."

64. Jesus is the river of life, flowing from the throne of God.

Revelation 22:1: "Then the angel showed me the river of the water of life, bright as crystal, flowing from the throne of God and of the Lamb."

65. Jesus is the rain that brings new life to dry ground.

Hosea 6:3: "Let us know; let us press on to know the Lord; his going out is sure as the dawn; he will come to us as the showers, as the spring rains that water the earth."

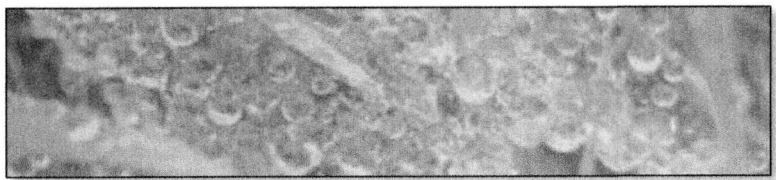

66. Jesus is the water that bears fruit.

Psalm 1:3: "He is like a tree planted by streams of water that yields its fruit in its season, and its leaf does not wither. In all that he does, he prospers."

67. Jesus is the river of peace.

Isaiah 66:12: "For thus says the Lord: 'Behold, I will extend peace to her like a river, and the glory of the nations like an overflowing stream; and you shall nurse, you shall be carried upon her hip, and bounced upon her knees."

68. Jesus is the well that never runs dry.

John 4:13-14: "Jesus said to her, 'Everyone who drinks of this water will be thirsty again, but whoever drinks of the water that I will give him will never be thirsty again. The water that I will give him will become in him a spring of water welling up to eternal life.'"

8 – JESUS AS THE LIVING WATER

69. Jesus is the fountain of life.

Psalm 36:9: "For with you is the fountain of life; in your light do we see light."

70. Jesus is the stream that cleanses.

Ephesians 5:26: "That he might sanctify her, having cleansed her by the washing of water with the word."

8 – JESUS AS THE LIVING WATER

In Summary:

61. **Jesus is the wellspring of life, refreshing my soul** (John 7:37-38).

62. **Jesus is the fountain of living water, quenching my thirst forever** (Jeremiah 2:13).

63. **Jesus is the water that makes the desert bloom** (Isaiah 35:6-7).

64. **Jesus is the river of life, flowing from the throne of God** (Revelation 22:1).

65. **Jesus is the rain that brings new life to dry ground** (Hosea 6:3).

66. **Jesus is the water that bears fruit** (Psalm 1:3).

67. **Jesus is the river of peace** (Isaiah 66:12).

68. **Jesus is the well that never runs dry** (John 4:13-14).

69. **Jesus is the fountain of life** (Psalm 36:9).

70. **Jesus is the stream that cleanses** (Ephesians 5:26).

9 - JESUS AS THE HEALER AND SAVIOR

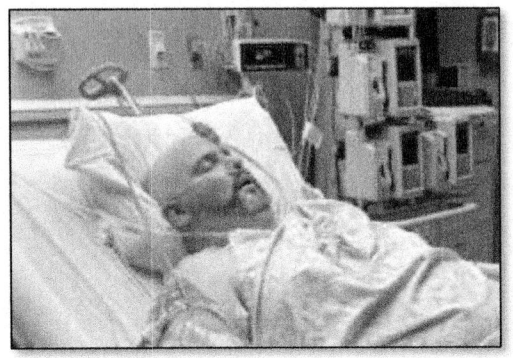

71. Jesus is the kind healer.

Psalm 41:1-3: "Blessed is the one who considers the poor! In the day of trouble the Lord delivers him; the Lord protects him and keeps him alive; he is called blessed in the land; you do not give him up to the will of his enemies. The Lord sustains him on his sickbed; in his illness, you restore him to full health."

72. Jesus is the one who binds up all of our wounds.

Psalm 147:3: "He heals the brokenhearted and binds up their wounds."

73. Jesus is the one who heals all of our diseases.

Psalm 103:3: "Who forgives all your iniquity, who heals all your diseases."

74. Jesus is the resurrection and the life.

John 11:25: "Jesus said to her, 'I am the resurrection and the life. Whoever believes in me, though he die, yet shall he live.'"

75. Jesus is the Anointed Healer and Deliverer.

Luke 4:18: "The Spirit of the Lord is upon me, because he has anointed me to proclaim good news to the poor. He has sent me to proclaim liberty to the captives and recovering of sight to the blind, to set at liberty those who are oppressed."

9 - JESUS AS THE HEALER AND SAVIOR

76. Jesus is the savior and the sinless one, who became sin for us.

2 Corinthians 5:21: "For our sake he made him to be sin who knew no sin, so that in him we might become the righteousness of God."

77. Jesus is the Lamb of God, who takes away the sin of the world.

Revelation 5:12: "Saying with a loud voice, 'Worthy is the Lamb who was slain, to receive power and wealth and wisdom and might and honor and glory and blessing!'"

78. Jesus is the Savior whose atoning sacrifice was made for our sins.

1 John 2:2: "He is the propitiation for our sins, and not for ours only but also for the sins of the whole world."

79. Jesus is the Savior who is the Overflowing Fountain of Mercy and Grace.

Titus 3:5-6: "He saved us, not because of works done by us in righteousness, but according to his own mercy, by the washing of regeneration and renewal of the Holy Spirit, whom he poured out on us richly through Jesus Christ our Savior."

80. Jesus is the Savior who paid the price for our freedom.

1 Timothy 2:6: "Who gave himself as a ransom for all, which is the testimony given at the proper time."

71. Jesus is the Kind Healer (Psalm 41:1-3).

72. Jesus is the One Who Binds Up All Our Wounds (Psalm 147:3).

73. Jesus is the One Who Heals All Our Diseases (Psalm 103:3).

74. Jesus is the Resurrection and the Life (John 11:25).

75. Jesus is the Anointed Healer and Deliverer (Luke 4:18).

76. Jesus is the Savior and the Sinless One, Who Became Sin for Us (2 Corinthians 5:21).

77. Jesus is the Lamb of God, Who Takes Away the Sin of the World (Revelation 5:12).

78. Jesus is the Savior Whose Atoning Sacrifice Was Made for Our Sins (1 John 2:2).

79. Jesus is the Overflowing Fountain of Mercy and Grace (Titus 3:5-6).

80. Jesus is the Savior Who Paid the Price for Our Freedom (1 Timothy 2:6).

10 - JESUS AS THE ALPHA AND OMEGA

81. Jesus is the Alpha and the Omega, the beginning and the end.

Revelation 22:13: "I am the Alpha and the Omega, the first and the last, the beginning and the end."

82. Jesus is the firstborn over all creation.

Colossians 1:15: "He is the image of the invisible God, the firstborn of all creation."

83. Jesus is the author and perfecter of our faith.

Hebrews 12:2: "Looking to Jesus, the founder and perfecter of our faith, who for the joy that was set before him endured the cross, despising the shame, and is seated at the right hand of the throne of God."

84. Jesus is the eternal one, who was and is and is to come.

Revelation 1:8: "I am the Alpha and the Omega," says the Lord God, "who is and who was and who is to come, the Almighty."

85. Jesus is the Head of the Church.

Colossians 1:18: "And he is the head of the body, the church. He is the beginning, the firstborn from the dead, that in everything he might be preeminent."

10 - JESUS AS THE ALPHA AND OMEGA

86. Jesus is the Unchanging One.

Hebrews 13:8: "Jesus Christ is the same yesterday and today and forever."

87. Jesus is the Word Who Was and Is and Is to Come.

John 1:1-2: "In the beginning was the Word, and the Word was with God, and the Word was God. He was in the beginning with God."

88. Jesus is the Author of Life.

Acts 3:15: "And you killed the Author of life, whom God raised from the dead. To this we are witnesses."

89. Jesus is the Cornerstone.

Ephesians 2:20: "Built on the foundation of the apostles and prophets, Christ Jesus himself being the cornerstone."

90. Jesus is the Eternal High Priest.

Hebrews 7:24-25: "But he holds his priesthood permanently, because he continues forever. Consequently, he is able to save to the uttermost those who draw near to God through him, since he always lives to make intercession for them."

In Summary:

81. **Jesus is the Alpha and the Omega, the beginning and the end** (Revelation 22:13).

82. **Jesus is the firstborn over all creation** (Colossians 1:15).

83. **Jesus is the author and perfecter of our faith** (Hebrews 12:2).

84. **Jesus is the eternal one, who was and is and is to come** (Revelation 1:8).

85. **Jesus is the Head of the Church** (Colossians 1:18).

86. **Jesus is the Unchanging One** (Hebrews 13:8).

87. **Jesus is the Word Who Was and Is and Is to Come** (John 1:1-2).

88. **Jesus is the Author of Life** (Acts 3:15).

89. **Jesus is the Cornerstone** (Ephesians 2:20).

90. **Jesus is the Eternal High Priest** (Hebrews 7:24-25).

11 - JESUS AS THE VICTOR AND HOPE

91. Jesus is the victorious warrior, defeating sin and death.

Revelation 19:11: "Then I saw heaven opened, and behold, a white horse! The one sitting on it is called Faithful and True, and in righteousness he judges and makes war."

92. Jesus is the overcomer, and in Him, I have victory.

1 Corinthians 15:57: "But thanks be to God, who gives us the victory through our Lord Jesus Christ."

93. Jesus is the name above every name, before which every knee will bow.

Philippians 2:8-11: "And being found in human form, he humbled himself by becoming obedient to the point of death, even death on a cross. Therefore God has highly exalted him and bestowed on him

the name that is above every name, so that at the name of Jesus every knee should bow, in heaven and on earth and under the earth, and every tongue confess that Jesus Christ is Lord, to the glory of God the Father."

94. Jesus is the one who holds the keys of death and Hades.

Revelation 1:18: "And the living one. I died, and behold I am alive forevermore, and I have the keys of Death and Hades."

95. Jesus is the mighty one, who saves.

Zephaniah 3:17: "The Lord your God is in your midst, a mighty one who will save; he will rejoice over you with gladness; he will quiet you by his love; he will exult over you with loud singing."

96. Jesus is my Eternal Hope.

1 Peter 1:21: "Who through him are believers in God, who raised him from the dead and gave him glory, so that your faith and hope are in God."

97. Jesus is the anchor of my soul, firm and secure.

Hebrews 6:19: "We have this as a sure and steadfast anchor of the soul, a hope that enters into the inner place behind the curtain."

98. Jesus is my living hope, who will never fade.

1 Peter 1:3-4: "Blessed be the God and Father of our Lord Jesus Christ! According to his great mercy, he has caused us to be born again to a living hope through the resurrection of Jesus Christ from the dead, to an inheritance that is imperishable, undefiled, and unfading, kept in heaven for you."

99. Jesus Chris is our Hope.

1 Timothy 1:1: "Paul, an apostle of Christ Jesus by command of God our Savior and of Christ Jesus our hope."

100. Jesus is the Faithful and True Witness.

Revelation 3:14: "And to the angel of the church in Laodicea write: 'The words of the Amen, the faithful and true witness, the beginning of God's creation.'"

In Summary:

91. **Jesus is the victorious warrior, defeating sin and death** (Revelation 19:11).

92. **Jesus is the overcomer, and in Him, I have victory** (1 Corinthians 15:57).

93. **Jesus is the name above every name, before which every knee will bow** (Philippians 2:8-11).

94. **Jesus is the one who holds the keys of death and Hades** (Revelation 1:18).

95. **Jesus is the mighty one, who saves** (Zephaniah 3:17).

96. **Jesus is our Eternal Hope** (1 Peter 1:21).

97. **Jesus is the anchor of my soul, firm and secure** (Hebrews 6:19).

98. **Jesus is my living hope, who will never fade** (1 Peter 1:3-4).

99. **Jesus Christ is our Hope** (1 Timothy 1:1).

100. **Jesus is the Faithful and True Witness** (Revelation 3:14).

12 - ABOUT THE AUTHOR

Sean Shetler is a U.S. Army Veteran, having served two deployments in Iraq totaling 26 months, and is a recipient of the Bronze Star Medal. Currently, he is a graduate student at Houston Christian University, pursuing a Master of Arts in Theological Studies (MATS)

with the ultimate goal of becoming a Hospital Chaplain. If God permits, he plans to continue his studies at the doctoral level.

Sean and his wife, Libni "Libby" Shetler, are actively involved in ministry at First Baptist Church of Marble Falls, Texas, where they serve as greeters. Sean also sings bass in the Contemporary Choir, while Libby, originally from Fortaleza, Ceará, Brazil, contributes her mezzo-soprano voice to both the Contemporary Choir and the Worship Team. Additionally, Sean works in audio-visual production at Refuge Church at the Mission Center, where he and Libby serve on the worship team every Thursday night in Marble Falls, Texas.

Beyond ministry, Sean and Libby are devoted to serving the homeless, poor, sick, refugees, and veterans, seeing their work as an extension of Christ's love and compassion. Sean is also passionate about writing, painting, photography, and evangelism, using his creative and artistic gifts to glorify God.

Sean's call to Chaplaincy was affirmed on Easter 2023, when he felt the Holy Spirit place this calling on his heart. His faith was further strengthened after a near-death experience (NDE) in January 2024, following complications from gastric sleeve surgery. This event deepened his resolve to serve others and honor God's calling on his life.

Together, Sean and Libby are raising their two wonderful children, Josiah Shetler (7) and Raelynn Noel Shetler (5), who bring them great joy and remind them of God's abundant grace.

Life Purpose Statement

"Our purpose is to live fully for Christ, understanding that to live is to serve Him and to die is to gain eternal reward. With every step, we run toward the goal of honoring God by dedicating ourselves to the well-being of others. We are committed to providing compassionate support and practical assistance to the poor, the homeless, veterans, refugees, and the oppressed. Through acts of kindness, advocacy, and service, we strive to uplift those in need and promote justice and dignity for all. Guided by our faith, we believe in the inherent worth of every individual (God does not show favoritism) and aim to embody God's love, empathy, and unwavering dedication in all our endeavors, so that He may receive all the glory."

Sean and Libby look forward to growing in faith, serving their community, and walking alongside others in their journey with Christ. May God bless you and fill your life with His peace, purpose, and presence!

Call to Ministry

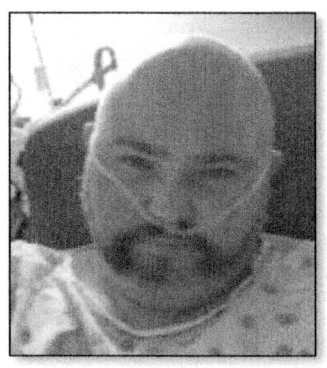

My spiritual journey has also led me to a clear calling to ministry. Since Easter 2023, I have felt a divine calling to serve as a Hospital Chaplain, a path that was profoundly affirmed through a life-altering experience. On January 23, 2024, I nearly died from internal bleeding following gastric sleeve surgery. I spent 4 days total in the hospital and intensive care unit (ICU) after losing 2.5 pints of blood and receiving more than 4 pints in transfusions. I experienced God's miraculous healing through the prayers of a chaplain named Casey, along with friends, family, and church members. Scriptures such as (**Psalm 41:1-4**), (**Psalm 103:3**) and (**Psalm 147:1-3**), which speak of God's healing power, now hold a deeply personal significance in my life. This experience strengthened my faith and confirmed my commitment to offering spiritual care, comfort, and encouragement to those in need.

Family and Community

On April 29, 2022, I married my wife, Libni ("Libby") Shetler, in Burnet, Texas, and our marriage was later registered in Brazil. Our union has been a profound blessing, bringing joy, companionship, and spiritual growth. On October 9, 2022, I had the privilege of baptizing my wife Libby at Connect Church in Liberty Hill, Texas, alongside Pastor Leighton Forshee, with Senior Pastor Dr. Danny Forshee in attendance.

In May 2023, we became members of First Baptist Church of Marble Falls, Texas, where Senior Pastor Dr. Ross Chandler has played a pivotal role in guiding our ministry. Through his leadership, we have been able to serve the poor, homeless, refugees, veterans, and families in crisis, living out our faith through acts of compassion and service.

Our faith journey has been enriched by our church community and our shared commitment to serve others. As I continue to grow spiritually, I draw inspiration from (**James 4:8**), which encourages drawing near to God and purifying one's heart. This verse encapsulates my ongoing journey of spiritual growth and development.

My spiritual journey has been a tapestry of faith, transformation, and service. Despite challenges and broken relationships, I find solace in God's unwavering support and guidance. My wife and I continue to seek ways to make a positive impact, driven by our shared faith and commitment to helping others.

Seminary Journey

Starting at the end of August 2024, I have now embarked on a new chapter in my spiritual and academic journey by pursuing a Master of Arts in Theology (MATS) online at Houston Christian University (formerly Houston Baptist University). I am now 1/3rd of the way complete with my degree program. This decision marks a significant step in my commitment to deepen my theological knowledge and prepare for a life of ministry.

Mentorship and Guidance

To support my seminary studies and spiritual growth, I will seek mentorship from two esteemed pastors at First Baptist Church of Marble Falls:

Family Discipleship Pastor Tucker Edwards: With his expertise in integrating faith and holistic well-being, Pastor Tucker will provide valuable guidance on maintaining a balanced and healthy approach to ministry.

Children's Pastor Nichole Sims: A recent Masters of Divinity Graduate of George W. Truett Seminary at Baylor University. Pastor Pastor Nichole will provide guidance on my spiritual formations and journey to becoming a Hospital Chaplain.

In addition to these mentors, I will regularly check in with Senior Pastor Dr. Ross Chandler. His leadership and experience will be instrumental in shaping my pastoral skills and ensuring that I stay grounded in my faith and committed to the calling God has placed on my life.

Goals and Aspirations

Pursuing a Masters of Arts in Theological Studies aka (MATS) is not just an academic endeavor for me; it is a response to the calling I have felt deeply since Easter of 2023. This calling was confirmed during a life-threatening experience on January 23, 2024, when I nearly died from internal bleeding after gastric sleeve surgery. The miraculous healing I experienced, supported by prayers from a chaplain, friends, family, and church members, reaffirmed my commitment to serve God through ministry. Additionally, a few months after my gastric surgery, I experienced complete healing from Type II Diabetes, as all symptoms were reversed.

As I embark on this seminary journey, my goals are clear:

Deepen Theological Understanding:

My goal is to gain a comprehensive understanding of Christian theology, biblical studies, and church history to effectively teach and preach the Word of God. I believe that God will grow the minister before he grows the ministry. The Holy Spirit is upon me for ministry and service. The Holy Spirit is in me for sanctification. The Holy Spirit is with me to bring me to Jesus. I believe that there are at least three important truths of the spiritual world. The unseen world shapes are lives more than what we realize. What fills my life determines my spiritual strength. True discipleship requires living in a spiritual reality that is taking place all around us.

Develop Pastoral Skills:

I am committed to honing my skills in pastoral care, counseling, and leadership to provide compassionate and effective ministry to those in need. My faith journey took a transformative turn when I was baptized on **Mother's Day 2019**, marking my dedication to Christ and the beginning of a deeper spiritual walk. Since that moment, I have grown in my understanding of Scripture, spiritual leadership, and God's calling on my life. Through seminary, ministry service, and personal experiences, I continue to develop the necessary skills to support, guide, and uplift those facing spiritual and personal challenges. My baptism was not the end but the beginning of a lifelong process of growth, as God continues to shape and equip me to serve others with wisdom, empathy, and unwavering faith.

Expand Ministry Outreach:

Learn strategies and best practices for mission work to serve the poor, homeless, refugees, veterans, and families in crisis, fulfilling the call to be the hands and feet of Christ in the world.

Foster Personal Spiritual Growth:

Continue to draw near to God, as (**James 4:8**) encourages, cleansing my hands and purifying my heart to be fully devoted to His service. Foster a deeper relationship with Christ through daily prayer, scripture study, and worship, allowing His presence to transform my heart and mind. Seek to grow in faith and wisdom, trusting in His guidance as I navigate both challenges and blessings. Cultivate a life of holiness and obedience, striving to reflect Christ's love in all that I do. Remain steadfast in my commitment to spiritual growth, knowing that true fulfillment is found in a closer walk with Him.

Sanctifying my thoughts is essential in growing closer to God, as (**Romans 12:2**) it instructs us: *"Do not be conformed to this world, but be transformed by the renewal of your mind, that by testing you may discern what is the will of God, what is good and acceptable and perfect."* (**Romans 12:2**) played a pivotal role in my journey to faith, serving as the verse that ultimately led me to surrender my life to Christ. Its call to be transformed by the renewal of my mind resonated deeply, compelling me to embrace Christianity, receive the Holy Spirit, and follow in obedience through baptism. This scripture continues to shape my walk with God, reminding me daily to seek His will and live a life set apart for His glory.

By meditating on His Word and fixing my mind on what is true, honorable, just, pure, lovely, and commendable (**Philippians 4:8**), I allow the Holy Spirit to shape my thoughts and align them with God's will. Sanctified thoughts lead to a transformed life, one that reflects Christ's character and glorifies Him in every action.

Keeping my mind focused on the things of God guards against temptation and strengthens my faith, allowing His peace to rule in my heart (**Colossians 3:15-16**).

Conclusion

My journey through seminary at Houston Christian University, supported by the mentorship of dedicated pastors and the guidance of Senior Pastor Dr. Ross Chandler, will equip me with the knowledge, skills, and spiritual depth needed for

effective ministry. I am excited and humbled by the opportunity to grow in my faith and to serve others in accordance with God's will.

As I continue this journey, I remain committed to deepening my understanding of God's Word and applying it in ways that bring hope and healing to those in need. My calling to chaplaincy is not just a career path but a sacred responsibility to offer comfort, encouragement, and spiritual guidance to the brokenhearted. Through my studies, ministry, and personal experiences, I strive to embody Christ's love and reflect His grace in all that I do. I am grateful for the unwavering support of my wife, family, mentors, and church community, who continue to uplift me in prayer and encouragement. Above all, I seek to glorify God in every step of this journey, trusting in His perfect plan. May my life and ministry be a testament to His faithfulness, love, and transforming power.

13 EPILOGUE

Book Review – Chapters 1-4 of Dr. Gailyn Van Rheenen's *Missions: Biblical Foundations and Contemporary Strategies*

The Biblical Narrative of Mission

(Chapter 1)

God is described as a missional and relational God. He is both the initiator and sustainer of mission, seeking to redeem His creation and restore relationship with humanity. His nature as a sending God is evident throughout the biblical narrative, from sending Abraham (**Genesis 12:1-3**) to sending His Son, Jesus (**John 3:16**), and the Holy Spirit (**John 14:26**). Understanding God as missional forms how we live by compelling us to align our lives with His mission, embodying His love and truth in our daily actions and relationships. We are called to participate in His redemptive work in the world, living as witnesses to His kingdom.

What aspects of God's nature motivate me to join Him in His mission?

God's compassionate and redemptive nature motivates me to join Him in His mission. His heart for the lost and the marginalized inspires action. For example, in (**Isaiah 61:1**), God speaks of binding up the brokenhearted and proclaiming freedom for the captives. Jesus echoes this in (**Luke 4:18-19**), proclaiming that He was anointed to bring good news to the poor. This compassion motivates me to engage in ministries that serve the homeless, refugees, and veterans, as seen in my volunteer work at the Mission Center, and share the gospel with those in need of hope.

Review the "I Am" Statements of Jesus. How does your belief in these statements motivate you to make Jesus known?

The "I am" statements of Jesus—such as "I am the bread of life" (**John 6:35**), "I am the light of the world" (**John 8:12**), and "I am the resurrection and the life" (**John 11:25**)—declare His divine identity and mission. These statements demonstrate Jesus' sufficiency to meet every need and provide eternal life. Belief in these truths compels me to make Jesus known, especially in contexts where people are searching for meaning, light, and hope. When I share about Jesus with others, I want them to experience Him as the One who truly satisfies, heals, and brings eternal life.

What is the central task to which the Great Commission (Matthew 28:18-20) calls us?

The central task of the Great Commission is to make disciples of all nations, baptizing them in the name of the Father, Son, and Holy Spirit, and teaching them to obey all that Jesus commanded. This involves evangelism, teaching, and training others to follow Christ in every aspect of life. The call is not just to convert people but to guide them into a life of discipleship, learning and living according to Jesus' teachings. The Commission emphasizes the global and inclusive nature of mission, inviting every follower of Jesus to participate in spreading the gospel to all peoples.

What was the "core gospel" that the Holy Spirit led Peter to proclaim at Pentecost?

The "core gospel" Peter proclaimed at Pentecost (**Acts 2:14-39**) was the message of Jesus' *life*, *death*, and *resurrection*. He declared that Jesus was crucified by lawless men but was raised from the dead by God, fulfilling the Scriptures. Peter emphasized Jesus as Lord and Messiah, urging the people to repent and be baptized for the forgiveness of sins and the gift of the Holy Spirit. This message was the foundation for the early church's mission, emphasizing both repentance and the transformative power of the resurrection.

13 EPILOGUE

In what sense was the conversion of Cornelius also part of the ongoing conversion of Peter and the church?

Cornelius' conversion (**Acts 10**) was part of Peter's and the church's ongoing conversion in the sense that it expanded their understanding of God's inclusivity in mission. Peter, a Jew, initially believed that the gospel was primarily for the Jews, but through the vision of the clean and unclean animals and the subsequent conversion of Cornelius, a Gentile, Peter realized that God shows no partiality (**Acts 10:34-35, Romans 2:11**). This event marked a significant shift in the church's mission, leading to the acceptance of Gentiles into the Christian community, breaking down ethnic and cultural barriers in spreading the gospel.

What was the role of the "apostolic band" in early Christian mission?

The "apostolic band" (i.e., the group of apostles and their close associates) played a foundational role in early Christian mission. They were eyewitnesses to Jesus' resurrection and were commissioned directly by Him to preach the gospel (**Acts 1:8**). Their role involved proclaiming the gospel, establishing churches, and teaching new believers. As leaders and pioneers, they traveled extensively to spread the gospel and ensure the doctrine remained faithful to Jesus' teachings, exemplified by Peter's leadership at Pentecost (**Acts 2**) and Paul's missionary journeys (**Acts 13-28**).

What did Paul hope the church in Rome would do for him after reading his grand exposition of "missional theology"?

After presenting his grand exposition of missional theology in **Romans**, Paul hoped that the church in Rome would support his mission to take the gospel to **Spain** (Romans 15:24). Paul envisioned the Roman church as a strategic partner in furthering the mission to the western reaches of the Roman Empire. He sought their practical support, including prayer, financial assistance, and possibly companionship on his journey. His desire was for the Roman church to become a base of operations for his continued missionary endeavors to unreached regions.

13 EPILOGUE

How is it that God's kingdom is "already" but "not yet" present? What is our task as believers during this in-between time?

God's kingdom is considered "already" present because, through Jesus' life, death, and resurrection, the reign of God has been inaugurated. Jesus proclaimed that the kingdom of God was at hand (Mark 1:15), and through His ministry, He demonstrated the power and presence of the kingdom by healing the sick, casting out demons, and forgiving sins. The kingdom is present wherever God's will is being done, and the Holy Spirit continues to work in the lives of believers to advance the kingdom through acts of love, justice, and reconciliation.

However, the kingdom is also "not yet" fully realized because the world still suffers under the effects of sin, death, and evil. While Jesus has defeated these forces through His resurrection, their complete eradication will occur only when Christ returns (Revelation 21:1-5). The "not yet" aspect of the kingdom points to the future fulfillment of God's reign, where there will be no more suffering, sin, or death.

During this in-between time, believers are called to **participate in God's mission** by being **witnesses of His kingdom** (Acts 1:8). Our task is to live as citizens of God's kingdom, embodying kingdom values such as justice, mercy, and humility (Micah 6:8). We are to share the gospel, make disciples, care for the marginalized, and work for peace and justice, all while waiting expectantly for the return of Christ. Our role is to live as "kingdom ambassadors" (2 Corinthians 5:20), representing God's kingdom in a broken world, while knowing that its full realization is yet to come.

What is the significance for you that mission is (*missio Dei*), the mission of God, and not a human endeavor?

The understanding that mission is *missio Dei*—the mission of God—rather than a human endeavor is deeply significant. It highlights that **God is the originator of mission**, and His purpose of redeeming and restoring creation is at the heart of all missional activity. This perspective gives great comfort and humility because it means that God is already at work in the world, and our role is to join Him in what He is doing. The burden of mission does not rest solely on human effort; instead, it is sustained by God's power and direction.

This understanding fosters **dependence on God** rather than on our own strategies or capabilities. For example, Jesus said in John 15:5, "Apart from me you can do nothing," which emphasizes that fruitful mission happens only through abiding in Christ. Recognizing mission as *missio Dei* ensures that we seek the guidance of the Holy Spirit, rely on prayer, and trust in God's sovereignty to accomplish His purposes (**Matthew 28:20**).

Furthermore, knowing that mission belongs to God encourages **perseverance and hope**. Even when we face challenges, setbacks, or resistance, we can trust that God's mission will not fail. As believers, we are privileged to participate in God's grand redemptive story, but ultimately, He is the one who brings the results. This truth inspires us to engage in mission with **humility, faith, and confidence**, knowing that it is God who equips us, directs us, and ensures that His kingdom will come fully in His time.

Application: When Jim and Julie learned the narrative of God's mission in Scripture, their lives where changed. In what ways have you been transformed? Specifically, what did you learn from (1) God's mission in the Old Testament, (2) God's mission through Jesus, and (3) God's mission in the church through his Holy Spirit? How does this chapter form your identity?

The narrative of God's mission in Scripture is deeply transformative because it provides a framework for understanding God's purpose in the world and how I can participate in it. Here's how I have been transformed by learning about God's mission in these three areas:

1. God's Mission in the Old Testament

In the Old Testament, I learned that God's mission began with His covenant with Abraham (**Genesis 12:1-3**), where He promised to bless all nations through Abraham's descendants. This showed me that God's heart has always been for all peoples, not just Israel. Additionally, God's concern for justice and righteousness is evident through the prophets, who repeatedly called Israel to care for the poor, the oppressed, and the marginalized (**Isaiah 58:6-7, Micah 6:8**). Seeing God's mission rooted in the Old Testament has transformed my understanding of justice as integral to the gospel and has motivated my work with the homeless, refugees, and veterans.

2. God's Mission Through Jesus

In Jesus, I see the full embodiment of God's mission. Jesus proclaimed the kingdom of God and demonstrated it through acts of healing, mercy, and redemption (**Luke 4:18-19**). His sacrificial death on the cross and resurrection revealed that God's mission involves not only restoration but also atonement for sin, making reconciliation between God and humanity possible. Jesus' compassion and His commitment to seek and save the lost (**Luke 19:10**) compel me to live a life of sacrificial love and evangelism. His example has inspired me to share the gospel with others and meet people's physical and spiritual needs.

3. God's Mission in the Church Through His Holy Spirit

The mission of God continues through the church, empowered by the Holy Spirit. After Jesus' ascension, the Holy Spirit was poured out on believers at Pentecost (**Acts 2**), empowering them to bear witness to Christ and spread the gospel to the ends of the earth. The Spirit continues to guide and equip the church to participate in God's mission today, giving us spiritual gifts and boldness to proclaim the gospel (**Acts 1:8**). Learning this has transformed my view of mission as a Spirit-led endeavor, reminding me to rely on prayer and the Spirit's guidance in all that I do for God's kingdom. This understanding gives me confidence and courage to engage in mission, knowing that the Spirit works through me.

4. How This Chapter Forms My Identity

This chapter shapes my identity by reinforcing the truth that I am part of God's ongoing mission. It challenges me to live with a missional mindset, understanding that my purpose is not just personal fulfillment but to be an *ambassador* for God's kingdom (**2 Corinthians 5:20**). The chapter reminds me that my life is part of a much larger story—the *missio Dei*, God's mission of redemption and restoration for all creation. This perspective influences how I prioritize my time, talents, and relationships, aligning my identity as a follower of Christ with a deep commitment to share His love and truth with the world. It forms in me a sense of purpose and responsibility to actively participate in God's redemptive work, both locally and globally.

II. Chapter 2 – Spiritual Awakenings for Mission (Page 61)

Reflection and Application

Questions:

1. Would you consider yourself a caterpillar, a pupa, or a butterfly? Why? How is God leading you to become a butterfly, one who is drawing nectar while spreading pollen?

I would consider myself a **pupa**—in a stage of transition and transformation. A caterpillar represents the early stages of faith, growing in knowledge and understanding. A butterfly represents a person fully living out their calling, spreading God's love and truth. As a pupa, I am in a period of spiritual growth, learning, and preparation, where God is reshaping my understanding and strengthening my heart for future ministry.

God is leading me to become a **butterfly** by teaching me to rely on His strength and wisdom, enabling me to **draw spiritual nourishment** from His Word and the Holy Spirit, while **spreading the gospel** through acts of service and discipleship. For example, volunteering at the Mission Center and evangelizing in the community are ways I am starting to share the nectar of God's love while spreading His transformative message.

2. Describe how Jesus moved from solitude to community to ministry. How could you employ this pattern practically in developing your daily rhythm of life?

Jesus often moved from **solitude** (prayer and communion with the Father), to **community** (fellowship with His disciples), and then to **ministry** (serving and teaching). We see this rhythm in (**Mark 1:35**), where Jesus prayed alone before engaging with the crowds and performing miracles. He regularly withdrew for solitude (**Luke 5:16**) but also invested deeply in His disciples and served the larger community.

Practically, I can follow this pattern by developing a **daily rhythm** that includes:

- **Solitude**: Setting aside time each morning for prayer, Scripture reading, and reflection to center my heart on God's mission.
- **Community**: Spending time with fellow believers in small groups or discipleship settings for mutual encouragement and accountability.
- **Ministry**: Engaging in service, whether through volunteer work or evangelism, to actively participate in God's kingdom work.

This rhythm allows me to stay grounded in God's presence while also fulfilling my calling to serve others.

3. What is the correlation between prayer and missions? Give a contemporary example of this relationship.

There is a direct correlation between **prayer and missions**. Prayer is the foundation of mission work because it aligns our hearts with God's will and empowers us through the Holy Spirit. Throughout Scripture, we see prayer as essential to the spread of the gospel. For example, in (**Acts 13:2-3**), the early church prayed and fasted before sending Paul and Barnabas on their missionary journey.

A contemporary example of this relationship can be seen in **global prayer movements** like the "24/7 Prayer" movement, which began in 1999 and has since inspired prayer initiatives worldwide. These movements have fueled mission work, leading to church planting, evangelistic efforts, and social justice initiatives across many nations.

4. Dave Davidson has written, "In our lifetime wouldn't it be sad if we spent more time washing dishes or swatting flies or mowing the yard or watching television than praying for world missions?" (2006). Realizing the truth of this statement, how should we reprioritize our time to give God space?

Dave Davidson's statement highlights the importance of **prioritizing prayer over mundane tasks**. While daily responsibilities like washing dishes and mowing the yard are necessary, we should intentionally carve out **time for prayer**—especially for world missions. To reprioritize our time, we can:

- Set aside **specific prayer times** each day, perhaps starting with 15 minutes dedicated solely to praying for missionaries, unreached people groups, and global needs.
- Replace certain non-essential activities, such as excessive TV watching or social media scrolling, with moments of intercession.
- Integrate prayer into daily routines, such as praying while doing household chores or exercising, to keep a constant connection with God.

By making these changes, we give God the space to work in our lives and the lives of others around the world.

5. Describe the role of colleges, universities, and Bible schools in the spiritual nurturing for world evangelization. Have such schools formed your passion and motivation for world missions? If so, how?

Colleges, universities, and Bible schools play a crucial role in fostering a deeper understanding of **world evangelization** by equipping students with both **theological knowledge** and **practical tools** for mission work. These institutions provide a structured environment where students can explore **biblical principles, theological concepts, and the history of the church's mission**, all of which are vital for engaging in global evangelization efforts.

In my pursuit of a **Master of Arts in Theological Studies (MATS)**, I have found that this program has greatly shaped my passion for world missions. The curriculum emphasizes **theological depth** while also encouraging students to think about how God's mission intersects with contemporary issues. Through studying topics such as **biblical theology, church history, and missiology**, I've gained a broader perspective on God's plan for humanity and how the church can engage in bringing the gospel to all nations.

Moreover, this academic journey has cultivated within me a stronger sense of **purpose and calling** in serving the marginalized, including the **homeless, addicts, veterans, and refugees**. The spiritual formation aspects of the program—such as prayer, reflection, and community engagement—have further developed my understanding that mission is not just about spreading the gospel, but about living it out through **compassionate service**. This holistic approach has inspired me to integrate my theological studies with practical outreach, motivating me to serve others in a way that reflects the heart of God's mission.

Application:

1. Outline a personal prayer and devotional pattern for your day. If you are married, you should develop these spiritual patterns with your spouse and children. What spiritually formative activities might you do in the morning, in the midday, in the evening?

Personal Prayer and Devotional Pattern

As a married person, establishing a consistent and intentional **prayer and devotional pattern** with my spouse is essential for our spiritual growth and unity. Here's a structured plan that includes spiritually formative activities throughout the day:

- **Morning:**
  - **Personal Devotion**: Start the day with individual prayer and Scripture reading, focusing on listening to God's voice and aligning my heart with His mission.
  - **Spousal Prayer**: Pray with my spouse, sharing our intentions for the day and asking God for guidance and protection over our family. We could also read a devotional together or meditate on a short passage.
  - **Family Prayer (if children are involved)**: Gather the family for a short prayer, teaching children to pray and reflect on a simple Bible verse that connects with their lives.

- **Midday:**
  - **Personal Reflection**: Pause for a moment of silent prayer or meditation during lunch, offering thanks and refocusing on God's presence amid daily activities.

- **Evening:**

    - **Scripture Meditation**: Read a short passage or verse to keep God's Word alive throughout the day and to realign with His mission.

  - **Evening:**

    - **Family Devotional**: Gather as a family to reflect on the day, offering prayers of gratitude and intercession for global missions, friends, and personal challenges.
    - **Spouse Devotion**: Before bed, spend time with my spouse in prayer, thanking God for His blessings and praying for the fulfillment of His mission in our lives.

This routine can help integrate **spiritual formation** into every part of the day, fostering both individual and family growth in faith.

2. Remember that spiritual formation is most effectively done with a community of faith. Define your role as God's person in your community of faith. How might an enhanced commitment to community guide you in your quest to know God and live out his missions in your life?

In my community of faith, my role is to be a **servant leader**, committed to embodying God's love, sharing His Word, and serving others. An **enhanced commitment to community** would involve:

- Actively participating in **small groups** or **discipleship programs** that foster accountability and spiritual growth.

- Using my **gifts** in teaching, mentoring, or serving to uplift others in their walk with Christ.

- Engaging in **outreach efforts** that align with God's mission, such as volunteering at the Mission Center and supporting global and local evangelization.

By being more deeply rooted in community, I am better equipped to learn from others, encourage fellow believers, and experience God's work in a more collective sense. **Living out God's mission** in a community sharpens my focus, reminds me of the bigger picture, and helps me embody **humility** and service in all areas of life.

3. Surf the Web to find references to the 1806 Haystack Prayer Meeting at Williams College. How could you put together your own prayer group for world evangelization?

The 1806 **Haystack Prayer Meeting** at Williams College was a significant event that birthed the American foreign missions movement. Five college students gathered under a haystack during a storm to pray for world evangelization, which later inspired the formation of the American Board of Commissioners for Foreign Missions.

To create my own prayer group for **world evangelization**, I would:

- **Identify a core group of like-minded believers** within my church or community who share a passion for missions.

- **Set regular meeting times**, either weekly or monthly, for prayer and reflection on global mission efforts.

- Focus on specific **unreached people groups**, missionaries, and countries, educating ourselves on their needs and praying for God's intervention.

- Encourage participants to **take action**, whether through supporting missions financially, going on mission trips, or volunteering locally.

This prayer group could become a space for **spiritual awakening** and mobilization for mission efforts, modeled after the Haystack Meeting's legacy.

4. The ancient church father Bernard of Clairvaux wrote, "Learn the lesson that, if you are to do the work of a prophet, what you need is not a scepter but a hoe." The kingly scepter symbolizes power and pride; the hoe signifies service and humility.

Bernard of Clairvaux's quote, "Learn the lesson that, if you are to do the work of a prophet, what you need is not a scepter but a hoe," emphasizes the need for **service** and **humility** in ministry. The **scepter** symbolizes power and authority, which can easily lead to pride, whereas the **hoe** represents the humble work of **cultivating** God's kingdom through service.

In my own life and ministry, this means embracing **servanthood**, focusing not on positions of power or recognition, but on faithfully doing the tasks that may seem small or unnoticed. Serving the homeless, veterans, and refugees is not about exercising authority but about **sowing seeds** of God's love through humble and compassionate acts. This approach fosters a mindset that prioritizes God's mission over personal ambition.

By wielding the **hoe of humility**, I align myself more fully with Christ's example of servant leadership (**Mark 10:45**), working quietly yet diligently to advance His kingdom.

III. Chapter 3 – Theological Foundations of Missions (Page 91)

Questions:

1. What metaphors describe a theology of mission? How do these metaphors help us understand the mission of God?

Metaphors such as **light**, **salt**, and **shepherding** describe a theology of mission:

- **Light:** Represents truth and revelation in a dark world (**Matthew 5:14**).

- **Salt:** Symbolizes preservation and flavor, highlighting the church's role in society (**Matthew 5:13**).

- **Shepherding:** Illustrates God's care and guidance (**John 10:11**). These metaphors help us understand God's mission as one of guidance, protection, and transformation in a fallen world.

2. How does understanding that God is the source of mission prepare our hearts for missions?

Recognizing that God is the source of mission prepares our hearts for missions by reminding us that it is not a human initiative but a divine calling. This understanding cultivates humility, reliance on

13 EPILOGUE

God's strength, and a commitment to align our efforts with His will, as seen in (**John 20:21**), where Jesus sends His disciples as the Father sent Him.

3. Tell the story of the mission of God in the life of one biblical character. How does this story spiritually form you as a person who wants to carry the mission of God?

Consider the life of **Moses**:

- **Call**: Moses is called by God at the burning bush (**Exodus 3**).

- **Mission**: He leads the Israelites out of Egypt, confronting Pharaoh and demonstrating God's power.

- **Formation**: Moses' story exemplifies obedience and faith in God's promises. It challenges me to embrace God's call, trusting in His provision, even amid uncertainty.

4. Use Scripture to define kingdom and the kingdom of God.

The **kingdom** refers to God's reign and authority, while the **kingdom of God** encompasses His sovereign rule over creation, manifesting in the lives of believers (**Luke 17:20-21**). It represents both a present reality and a future hope, as seen in (**Matthew 4:17**), where Jesus proclaims the kingdom's nearness.

(**Colossians 1:15-18**) presents a profound theological understanding of Christ's nature and His role in the Kingdom of God. Here's the passage from the ESV:

Colossians 1:15-18:

> "15 - He is the image of the invisible God, the firstborn of all creation. 16 - For by him all things were created, in heaven and on earth, visible and invisible, whether thrones or dominions or rulers or authorities— all things were created through him and for him. 17- And he is before all things, and in him all things hold together. 18- And he is the head of the body, the church. He is the beginning, the firstborn from the dead, that in everything he might be preeminent."

Connection to the Kingdom of God

1. ### Christ as the Image of God:

   - Verse 15 identifies Jesus as the "image of the invisible God." This emphasizes that Jesus reveals God's nature and character, essential for understanding God's Kingdom. The Kingdom of God is fundamentally about God's reign, and knowing Christ allows believers to grasp the nature of that reign.

2. ### Creation and Authority:

   - In Verse 16, Paul asserts that all things were created through and for Christ. This reinforces His authority over creation, including spiritual realms (thrones, dominions, rulers, authorities). The Kingdom of God is established under Christ's sovereign rule, indicating that His reign encompasses all aspects of creation, both physical and spiritual.

3. ### Sustainer of All Things:

   - Verse 17 states that "in him all things hold together." This suggests that Christ is not only the Creator but also the sustainer of creation. The Kingdom of God operates under His governance, ensuring order and purpose in the universe.

4. ### Head of the Church:

   - In Verse 18, Christ is described as the head of the body, the church. The church is central to the Kingdom of God, functioning as the community of believers who advance God's purposes on earth. Through the church, believers participate in the Kingdom's work, reflecting Christ's authority and mission.

5. ### Preeminence:

   - The term "preeminent" highlights Christ's supreme position in all things. This preeminence is foundational for understanding the Kingdom of God, where Christ's lordship is acknowledged and celebrated. His position as the "firstborn from the dead" also signifies the hope of resurrection and eternal life within the Kingdom.

Conclusion

(Colossians 1:15-18) beautifully encapsulates key aspects of the Kingdom of God by affirming Christ's authority, His role in creation and sustenance, and His leadership of the church. Understanding these verses enriches one's comprehension of what it means to live under the reign of Christ and participate in the unfolding of God's Kingdom on earth.

5. Why is kingdom living a countercultural lifestyle? How does living in the kingdom help you prioritize the decisions you make in life?

Kingdom living is countercultural because it often challenges societal norms, such as power dynamics, materialism, and individualism. Living in the kingdom helps prioritize decisions based on values like love, service, and justice (**Matthew 5:3-12**), guiding us to reflect Christ's character in our actions.

6. What is the meaning of the phrase "inaugurated eschatology"? Use this phrase to describe how Christians stand between the times.

Inaugurated eschatology refers to the belief that the kingdom of God has already begun through Jesus but will be fully realized in the future (**Hebrews 2:8**). Christians stand "between the times," living in the tension of the already (Christ's reign) and the not yet (future fulfillment).

7. How does a theology of the kingdom of God shape how we live and minister?

1. Theology of the Kingdom

A theology of the kingdom shapes our lives and ministries by motivating us to live out kingdom values, prioritize the marginalized, and engage in holistic mission (**Matthew 25:31-46**). It compels us to proclaim the gospel while addressing social

13 EPILOGUE

injustices.

A theology of the kingdom of God profoundly influences how we live and minister as Christians, shaping our understanding of our role in the world and our relationships with others. This theology emphasizes that the kingdom of God is not just a future hope but a present reality that calls us to embody its values in our daily lives. Here are several key aspects of how a theology of the kingdom shapes our actions and ministry:

2. Living Out Kingdom Values

Biblical Basis: (Matthew 5:3-12) (ESV)

"Blessed are the poor in spirit, for theirs is the kingdom of heaven. Blessed are those who mourn, for they shall be comforted... Blessed are the merciful, for they shall receive mercy."

A theology of the kingdom invites us to embody the values exemplified in the Sermon on the Mount. These values—humility, mercy, peacemaking, and justice—become the guiding principles for our lives and ministries. By living out these qualities, we reflect the character of Christ and demonstrate the reality of the kingdom to those around us.

3. Prioritizing the Marginalized

Biblical Basis: (Luke 4:18-19) (ESV)

"The Spirit of the Lord is upon me, because he has anointed me to proclaim good news to the poor. He has sent me to proclaim liberty to the captives and recovering of sight to the blind, to set at liberty those who are oppressed..."

A kingdom theology compels us to prioritize the marginalized and oppressed, recognizing that Jesus' ministry focused on those who were often overlooked or marginalized by society. This prioritization leads us to engage in advocacy, service, and support for the poor, refugees, the homeless, and other vulnerable populations. By aligning our ministries with God's heart for justice, we participate in the work of the kingdom and reflect God's love and compassion.

4. Engaging in Holistic Mission

Biblical Basis: **(Matthew 25:31-46)** (ESV)

"Then the King will say to those on his right, 'Come, you who are blessed by my Father, inherit the kingdom prepared for you from the foundation of the world. For I was hungry and you gave me food, I was thirsty and you gave me drink, I was a stranger and you welcomed me...'"

A theology of the kingdom encourages a holistic approach to mission that addresses both spiritual and physical needs. This includes evangelism, discipleship, and social justice work. By caring for the whole person, we reflect the comprehensive nature of the kingdom of God. Our ministries should encompass acts of compassion, justice, and advocacy, as well as the proclamation of the gospel, demonstrating the fullness of God's love and concern for humanity.

5. Proclaiming the Gospel

Biblical Basis: **(Mark 16:15)** (ESV)

"And he said to them, 'Go into all the world and proclaim the gospel to the whole creation.'"

A kingdom theology emphasizes the importance of proclaiming the gospel as a central aspect of our ministry. Sharing the good news of Jesus Christ is not only about individual salvation but also about inviting people to be part of the kingdom community, where they can experience transformation, healing, and reconciliation. This proclamation should be accompanied by authentic relationships and community engagement, demonstrating the reality of the kingdom in action.

6. Living with Hope and Expectation

Biblical Basis: **(Revelation 21:1-4)** (ESV)

"Then I saw a new heaven and a new earth, for the first heaven and the first earth had passed away, and the sea was no more... And I heard a loud voice from the throne saying, 'Behold, the dwelling place of God is with man. He will dwell with them, and they will be his people, and God himself will be with them as their God...'"

A theology of the kingdom instills in us a sense of hope and expectation for the future, as we anticipate the ultimate fulfillment of God's kingdom. This passage of Scripture resonated with me when I was laying in the Intensive Care Unit (ICU). During my near death experience (NDE) I saw what is depicted in (**Revelation 21**).This hope shapes our present actions, motivating us to work towards justice, peace, and reconciliation. It assures us that our labor in the kingdom is not in vain and that we are part of a larger narrative that will culminate in God's ultimate restoration of creation.

7. Building Community and Relationships

Biblical Basis: (Acts 2:44-47) (ESV)

"And all who believed were together and had all things in common... And the Lord added to their number day by day those who were being saved."

A theology of the kingdom fosters a sense of community and belonging among believers. It encourages us to live in authentic relationships characterized by love, support, and mutual accountability. By building a kingdom-oriented community, we create spaces where people can experience God's love and grace, fostering an environment where the gospel can flourish.

Conclusion

In summary, a theology of the kingdom of God profoundly shapes our lives and ministries by calling us to live out kingdom values, prioritize the marginalized, engage in holistic mission, proclaim the gospel, and build authentic community. It reminds us that our actions have eternal significance as we work to reflect God's love, justice, and grace in a world that desperately needs it. As we live out this theology, we participate in the unfolding of God's kingdom on earth, bringing hope and transformation to our communities.

8. Use Scripture to define incarnation.

Incarnation refers to God becoming flesh in the person of Jesus Christ (**John 1:14**). This doctrine emphasizes the mystery of God dwelling among humanity, revealing His nature and purpose.

13 EPILOGUE

The doctrine of the incarnation is central to Christian theology, emphasizing the mystery of God becoming flesh in the person of Jesus Christ. Here are several verses that further describe the incarnation and its significance:

Key Scriptures on the Incarnation

1. **John 1:14** (ESV)

   "And the Word became flesh and dwelt among us, and we have seen his glory, glory as of the only Son from the Father, full of grace and truth."

   This foundational verse highlights the core of the incarnation, where the eternal Word (Logos) takes on human form and lives among humanity.

2. **Philippians 2:6-8** (ESV)

   "Who, though he was in the form of God, did not count equality with God a thing to be grasped, but emptied himself, by taking the form of a servant, being born in the likeness of men. And being found in human form, he humbled himself by becoming obedient to the point of death, even death on a cross."

   This passage emphasizes Christ's humility and the voluntary nature of His incarnation, showcasing His obedience and sacrificial love.

3. **Colossians 1:19** (ESV)

   "For in him all the fullness of God was pleased to dwell."

   This verse affirms the fullness of God's presence in Christ, illustrating that Jesus embodies the complete nature of God.

4. **Hebrews 2:14-17** (ESV)

   "Since therefore the children share in flesh and blood, he himself likewise partook of the same things, that through death he might destroy the one who has the power of death, that is, the devil, and deliver all those who through fear of death were subject to lifelong slavery. For surely it is not angels that he helps, but he helps the offspring of Abraham. Therefore he had to be made like his brothers in every respect, so that he might become a merciful and faithful high priest in the service of God."

This passage highlights the necessity of Christ's incarnation, emphasizing His solidarity with humanity and His role as a compassionate high priest.

5. **Matthew 1:23** (ESV)

   "Behold, the virgin shall conceive and bear a son, and they shall call his name Immanuel (which means, God with us)."

   This verse connects the incarnation with the prophetic announcement of Jesus' birth, affirming that He is indeed "God with us."

6. **1 John 4:2** (ESV)

   "By this you know the Spirit of God: every spirit that confesses that Jesus Christ has come in the flesh is from God."

   This passage emphasizes the importance of acknowledging the incarnation as a test of true belief, reinforcing its significance in the Christian faith.

7. **Luke 1:35** (ESV)

   "And the angel answered her, 'The Holy Spirit will come upon you, and the power of the Most High will overshadow you; therefore the child to be born will be called holy—the Son of God.'"

   This verse describes the miraculous conception of Jesus, emphasizing His divine origin and the role of the Holy Spirit in the incarnation.

8. **John 10:30** (ESV)

"I and the Father are one."

This statement from Jesus affirms His unity with the Father, illustrating the divine nature of His incarnation.

9. **Romans 8:3** (ESV)

"For God has done what the law, weakened by the flesh, could not do. By sending his own Son in the likeness of sinful flesh and for sin, he condemned sin in the flesh."

This verse emphasizes that Jesus came in the likeness of humanity to address the problem of sin, fulfilling the law's purpose.

10. **Galatians 4:4-5** (ESV)

"But when the fullness of time had come, God sent forth his Son, born of woman, born under the law, to redeem those who were under the law, so that we might receive adoption as sons."

This passage illustrates the divine timing of the incarnation and its purpose in God's redemptive plan for humanity.

Conclusion

The incarnation is a profound mystery that reveals God's heart and purpose in coming to humanity as Jesus Christ. These scriptures collectively underscore the significance of the incarnation in understanding God's nature, His desire for relationship with humanity, and His redemptive work through Christ.

9. Describe how a theology of incarnation shapes practical missionary life and ministry.

A theology of incarnation shapes missionary life by modeling the importance of presence, relationship, and empathy. Just as Jesus engaged with people in their contexts, we are called to immerse ourselves in the lives of those we serve, embodying the love of Christ (Philippians 2:5-8).

10. Use Scripture to define a theology of the cross (a theology of crucifixion and resurrection).

A theology of the cross encompasses both crucifixion and resurrection, emphasizing sacrifice, redemption, and hope (1 Corinthians 1:18). It highlights that through Christ's death, believers are reconciled to God and empowered for new life.

A theology of the cross, which encompasses both the crucifixion and resurrection of Jesus Christ, is foundational to Christian belief. It highlights the significance of Christ's suffering, sacrifice, and victory over death, and can be defined and illustrated through various Scriptures. Here are some key elements and examples of Christology that inform this theology:

1. The Crucifixion as Atonement for Sin

Key Scripture: Isaiah 53:5 (ESV)

"But he was pierced for our transgressions; he was crushed for our iniquities; upon him was the chastisement that brought us peace, and with his wounds, we are healed."

This verse illustrates the belief that Christ's suffering and death were necessary for the atonement of sin, fulfilling the prophecy of a suffering servant. It emphasizes that through His wounds, humanity receives healing and forgiveness.

2. The Resurrection as Victory over Death

Key Scripture: 1 Corinthians 15:55-57 (ESV)

"O death, where is your victory? O death, where is your sting? The sting of death is sin, and the power of sin is the law. But thanks be to God, who gives us the victory through our Lord Jesus Christ."

The resurrection signifies Christ's victory over sin and death, offering hope for eternal life to believers. This transformation from death to life is central to the Christian faith and a cornerstone of Christology.

3. The Cross as Revelation of God's Love

Key Scripture: Romans 5:8 (ESV)

"But God shows his love for us in that while we were still sinners, Christ died for us."

The Greek word for "to die" used in Romans 5:8 is "ἀποθνῄσκω" (apothnēskō), which appears 111 times in the New Testament. Interestingly, the number 111 is often associated with the symbol of the Trinity. The phrase "Christ died for us," captured in four Greek words, beautifully summarizes the *gospel*. This verb means "to die" or "to be put to death," and is used throughout the New Testament to describe physical death or the end of life. [12]

In Romans 5:8, it is part of the passage: "But God shows his love for us in that while we were still sinners, *Christ died for us*." This verse highlights the cross as the ultimate demonstration of God's love for humanity. It underscores the idea that Christ's sacrificial death was not just a historical event but a profound expression of divine love and grace.

4. Christ as the Lamb of God

Key Scripture: John 1:29 (ESV)

"The next day he saw Jesus coming toward him, and said, 'Behold, the Lamb of God, who takes away the sin of the world!'"

This passage emphasizes Jesus' role as the sacrificial lamb, fulfilling the Old Testament sacrificial system. It connects the theology of the cross to the broader narrative of salvation history.

---

[12] The Greek word "ἀποθνῄσκω" (apothnēskō), meaning "to die" (Strong's # 599), appears 111 times in the New Testament. See William D. Mounce, *Mounce's Complete Expository Dictionary of Old and New Testament Words* (Grand Rapids, MI: Zondervan, 2006), 1092.

5. Identification with Humanity's Suffering

Key Scripture: Philippians 2:7-8 (ESV)

"But emptied himself, by taking the form of a servant, being born in the likeness of men. And being found in human form, he humbled himself by becoming obedient to the point of death, even death on a cross."

This verse illustrates the incarnation and humility of Christ, identifying with human suffering. It demonstrates that Jesus willingly embraced the cross, modeling obedience and servanthood.

6. The Cross as a Call to Discipleship

Key Scripture: Luke 9:23 (ESV)

"And he said to all, 'If anyone would come after me, let him deny himself and take up his cross daily and follow me.'"

This passage reflects the call to discipleship, where believers are invited to participate in the suffering and sacrifice of Christ. It signifies that the cross is not only a historical event but also a personal commitment for followers of Christ.

Examples of Christology

1. **High Christology**: This perspective emphasizes the divinity of Christ, often focusing on His pre-existence and role as Creator.

    Key Scripture: John 1:1-3 (ESV) – "In the beginning was the Word, and the Word was with God, and the Word was God."

2. **Low Christology**: This perspective emphasizes the humanity of Christ, focusing on His experiences, suffering, and relationships.

    Key Scripture: Hebrews 4:15 (ESV) – "For we do not have

a high priest who is unable to sympathize with our weaknesses, but one who in every respect has been tempted as we are, yet without sin."

3. **Christ as Prophet**: Reflects Jesus' role in proclaiming God's truth and revealing His will.

    Key Scripture: Luke 4:18-19 (ESV) – "The Spirit of the Lord is upon me, because he has anointed me to proclaim good news to the poor..."

4. **Christ as Priest**: Illustrates His mediatory role and sacrificial service.

    Key Scripture: Hebrews 7:24-25 (ESV) – "But he holds his priesthood permanently, because he continues forever. Consequently, he is able to save to the uttermost those who draw near to God through him..."

5. **Christ as King**: Affirms Jesus' authority and sovereignty.

    Key Scripture: Revelation 19:16 (ESV) – "On his robe and on his thigh he has a name written, King of kings and Lord of lords."

7. Conclusion

A theology of the cross encompasses the sacrificial death and victorious resurrection of Jesus Christ. It reveals God's profound love and justice while offering believers hope for redemption and eternal life. Through various Christological perspectives, we can better understand the multifaceted identity and mission of Jesus, who embodies both the divine and human, inviting us to follow Him in our own journeys of faith.

11. How does this theology of the cross shape how we live and minister?

The theology of the cross profoundly shapes our lives and ministries by presenting a framework for understanding our identity and purpose as followers of Christ. Central to this theology is the understanding that Jesus' suffering, crucifixion, and ultimate resurrection are not only historical events but also models for how we are called to live and minister in the world today.

1. Embracing Suffering and Sacrifice:

The theology of the cross teaches us that suffering is an integral part of the Christian experience. Romans 12:1 urges us to present our bodies as living sacrifices, holy and pleasing to God. This call to sacrifice reflects the heart of Christ, who willingly endured the cross for our salvation. As we embrace our own sufferings—whether through personal trials or the burdens of those we serve—we develop a deeper empathy and compassion that enhances our ministry. We become vessels of God's love, demonstrating that even in pain and hardship, there is hope and purpose.

2. Humility and Servanthood:

The cross embodies humility, as Jesus, in His divine nature, chose to serve rather than to be served. Philippians 2:5-8 reminds us to have the same mindset as Christ, who humbled Himself to the point of death. This humility calls us to view ourselves as servants within our communities, prioritizing the needs of others over our own desires. In ministry, this might mean stepping into uncomfortable situations or serving those who are marginalized and overlooked. By modeling servanthood, we not only follow Christ's example but also create an inviting atmosphere where others can encounter God's love.

3. Strength in Weakness:

The theology of the cross challenges conventional notions of strength and success. 2 Corinthians 12:9-10 states that God's power is made perfect in weakness. This paradox allows us to recognize that our limitations and struggles can become opportunities for God to work through us. In our ministries, we may face challenges that feel overwhelming, but it is in these moments that we learn to depend on God's grace and strength. Our testimonies of relying on God in difficult times can inspire others and draw them closer to Him.

4. Proclaiming Hope and Redemption:

The cross is not just a symbol of suffering; it is also the gateway to resurrection and new life. This duality shapes our message in ministry. While we acknowledge and address the pain and brokenness in our world, we also proclaim the hope found in Christ's victory over sin and death. This hope encourages us to be agents of reconciliation, bringing healing and restoration to individuals and communities. Our ministry becomes a reflection of the transformative power of the gospel, inviting others to experience the abundant life that Christ offers.

5. Community and Accountability:

Living out the theology of the cross also emphasizes the importance of community. We are called to bear one another's burdens (Galatians 6:2), creating a supportive environment where individuals can share their struggles and victories. Accountability within the church fosters spiritual growth and resilience, enabling us to navigate the challenges of life and ministry together. As we walk alongside one another, we reflect the unity of the body of Christ, demonstrating the love and grace that stem from the cross.

Conclusion

In summary, the theology of the cross shapes our lives and ministries by calling us to embrace suffering and sacrifice, embody humility and servanthood, find strength in weakness, proclaim hope and redemption, and cultivate a supportive community. By aligning our lives with the principles of the cross, we become effective witnesses of Christ's love and grace in a world desperately in need of both.

Application:

Creatively outline, draw, or diagram the biblical story line of the mission Dei (Page 70).

13 EPILOGUE

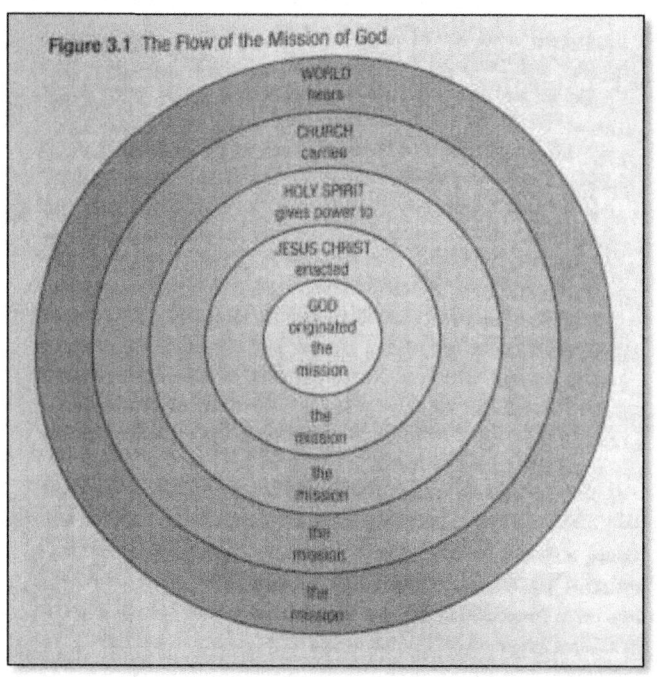

Personal Inventory:

How has God spoken to you through this chapter? What is God calling you to do about it?

Reflecting on how God has spoken to you through a particular chapter can be a deeply personal and transformative experience. Here are some guiding questions and points to consider that might help you articulate your thoughts:

1. Understanding God's Voice

Reflection: In what ways do you feel God has communicated specific truths or insights to you through this chapter? Were there particular verses, concepts, or examples that resonated with your current situation?

Application: How can you discern God's voice amidst the distractions of daily life? What practices (like prayer, meditation, or journaling) can help you cultivate a deeper awareness of His guidance?

2. Conviction and Change

Reflection: Did this chapter challenge any existing beliefs or attitudes you hold? Are there areas of your life where you feel convicted to change or grow?

Application: What specific changes is God prompting you to make? Consider actions that align with the insights gained—perhaps a shift in your priorities, relationships, or ministry focus.

3. Call to Action

Reflection: What is God specifically calling you to do in response to the truths presented in the chapter? Are there particular individuals, communities, or issues that you feel led to engage with?

Application: Create a tangible action plan. This could include committing to serve those in need, sharing the gospel with someone, or advocating for justice in your community.

4. Empowerment through Prayer

Reflection: How can prayer be a means of responding to God's call? Did the chapter inspire you to seek God more earnestly for guidance, strength, or clarity?

Application: Develop a prayer strategy. This may involve specific prayers for wisdom in decision-making or for opportunities to live out the truths you've learned.

5. Building Community

Reflection: How does the message of the chapter relate to your involvement in your church or community? Are there ways to engage others in the journey you are on?

Application: Consider reaching out to fellow believers for accountability and support. This could be through study groups, volunteering, or starting discussions about the themes in the chapter.

Conclusion

Take time to write down your reflections, and consider sharing them with someone you trust—this could deepen your understanding and commitment to act on what you've learned. Ultimately, the goal is to move from insight to action, allowing God's truth to shape your life and the lives of those around you. Remember that responding to God's call is a journey, and each step you take in faith is significant.

Example Personal Inventory: Completed

Personal Inventory

1. Understanding God's Voice

Reflection:

In this chapter, I sensed God communicating a profound truth about His love and grace. The verse from Ephesians 2:8-9, which reminds us that we are saved by grace through faith, resonated deeply with my current situation as I navigate my personal challenges and uncertainties in life. This truth reassured me that my worth is not based on my performance but on God's unconditional love.

Application:

To discern God's voice amidst distractions, I can commit to daily quiet time in prayer and reflection. For instance, I will set aside 15 minutes each morning to read Scripture and journal my thoughts, which will help cultivate a deeper awareness of His guidance throughout the day.

2. Conviction and Change

Reflection:

This chapter challenged me to examine my beliefs about forgiveness. I realized I often hold onto grudges instead of extending grace to others. I feel convicted to change my attitude toward [specific person or situation] where I have struggled to forgive.

Application:

God is prompting me to make specific changes, including reaching out to [insert name] and expressing my desire to reconcile. I plan to prioritize forgiveness in my relationships and actively work on letting go of past hurts by praying for the strength to do so.

3. Call to Action

Reflection:
I believe God is calling me to engage more actively in my community, particularly regarding the needs of the homeless

population in my area. I feel led to organize a food drive and volunteer at the local shelter.

Application:

I will create a tangible action plan that includes coordinating with my church to host a food drive in the coming month. I will also commit to volunteering at the shelter every other Saturday to serve meals and provide support to those in need.

4. Empowerment through Prayer

Reflection:

Prayer has become a crucial means of responding to God's call. This chapter inspired me to seek Him more earnestly for guidance, especially as I navigate new opportunities in my ministry.

Application:

I will develop a prayer strategy that includes praying for wisdom in decision-making regarding my ministry and for clarity on how to serve others effectively. Specifically, I'll set aside time each week to pray for the needs of my community and for opportunities to share the gospel.

5. Building Community

Reflection:

The message of this chapter has encouraged me to reflect on my involvement in my church. I see opportunities to engage others by starting a discussion group focused on service and outreach initiatives.

Application:

I will reach out to fellow believers for accountability and support by initiating a monthly meeting where we can discuss ways to serve our community. I plan to invite a few friends to join me in brainstorming ideas and forming a plan for our outreach efforts.

Conclusion

I will take time to write down my reflections and share them with my wife, as I believe her support will deepen my understanding and commitment. My ultimate goal is to move from insight to action, allowing God's truth to shape my life and the lives of those around me. Responding to God's call is a journey, and I am grateful for each step I can take in faith.

IV. Chapter 4 – The Church (Page 105-106)

Refection and Application

Questions:

1. What is the significance of each statement below in describing the relationship between the church and mission?

A. "The Church is the result of mission."

This statement highlights that the church exists because of God's initiative to reach out to humanity. Mission precedes the church; it was God's plan to create a community of believers who would reflect His love and serve His purpose in the world. The church's identity is rooted in the mission of God, emphasizing that its primary role is to fulfill this mission by proclaiming the gospel and making disciples.

B. "For the church to effectively minister, it must be God's distinctive people in the world."

This statement emphasizes that the church must embody the character and values of God to have a genuine impact. Being God's distinctive people means living in a way that reflects His holiness, love, and justice, which sets the church apart from secular culture. Effective ministry arises from a community that is not only distinct but also actively engages in the world with the transformative power of the gospel.

C. "The church most frequently establishes its rationale for being -its purpose for existing - white articulating its faith. An unexpressed faith withers."

This statement underlines the importance of expressing faith through teaching, preaching, and communal life. A church that does not articulate its beliefs risks becoming stagnant and losing its sense of purpose. By clearly communicating its faith, the church nurtures its members, inspires action, and draws others to Christ, ensuring that its mission remains vibrant and relevant.

D. "The purpose of the church is not merely to interpret history but also to become God's instrument for shaping the future he intends for the world."

This statement signifies that the church is called to actively participate in God's redemptive plan. Rather than merely reflecting on past events, the church is tasked with engaging in the present and future work of God. This involves addressing social injustices, advocating for the marginalized, and fostering hope, ultimately leading to a future aligned with God's kingdom.

2. How do you think your church is perceived by its non-Christian neighbors? How would you know?

I believe First Baptist Church of Marble Falls may be perceived by its non-Christian neighbors as a welcoming and supportive community. Many people in our area recognize the church as a place where individuals come together to find encouragement and assistance. This perception can be gauged through various means, such as community surveys, feedback from local outreach efforts, and informal conversations with neighbors during community events.

To further understand how we are viewed, we can engage with the community through events like food drives, holiday celebrations, and service projects, which would not only provide valuable insights into their feelings toward the church but also strengthen relationships within the community. By actively participating in the lives of our neighbors and addressing their needs, we can enhance our reputation as a loving and approachable church.

3. Contrast how the world sees itself with how the church molded by the mission of God sees the world. How do

Christians live "in the world" yet not be "of the world" (John 17:14-16)?

The world often sees itself through the lens of individualism, self-interest, and materialism, emphasizing personal gain and societal status. In contrast, the church, molded by the mission of God, sees the world as a place for stewardship, service, and witness to God's love and grace. While Christians live "in the world," they are called to be distinct by embodying the values of Christ—serving others, promoting justice, and loving their neighbors as themselves (Matthew 22:39). Living "not of the world" (John 17:14-16) means that Christians should not conform to societal norms that contradict God's principles but instead demonstrate a countercultural lifestyle rooted in faith, hope, and love.

4. What is the significance of the question, "What does it mean for the church to live under the cross?"

The question, "What does it mean for the church to live under the cross?" is significant because it emphasizes the foundational aspect of the cross in Christian identity and mission. Living under the cross means embracing humility, sacrifice, and a commitment to service, reflecting Christ's self-giving love. It challenges the church to prioritize the needs of others over personal desires and to engage in a ministry that acknowledges suffering and injustice in the world. This perspective drives the church to be a witness of hope and reconciliation, demonstrating that true strength is found in weakness and that life comes through death, mirroring the redemptive work of Christ.

Application:

1. Talk to someone who knows how your congregation began and write a paragraph summarizing the story.

A. Summary of the Church's Beginnings:

First Baptist Church of Marble Falls has a rich history that reflects the faith and commitment of its founding members. The church began in the early 1900s, driven by a group of believers who desired to create a place of worship in the growing community. They held their first services in a small building, where they gathered to pray, worship, and study the Scriptures. Over the years, the church has evolved, expanding its facilities and ministries to meet the needs of the congregation and the community. Today, First Baptist Church continues to uphold its foundational mission of sharing the gospel and serving others, embodying the love of Christ in Marble Falls.

2. Ask three non-Christians what words they would use to describe people who follow Christ. If their descriptions are negative, don't argue but ask forgiveness. Write a short description of your experience.

B. Experience with Non-Christians:

In my conversations with three non-Christians, I asked them what words they would use to describe people who follow Christ. Their responses included "hypocritical," "judgmental," and "self-righteous." While these descriptions were disheartening, I approached the discussion with an open heart, listening to their perspectives without being defensive. I acknowledged their feelings and expressed my sincere apologies if any negative experiences with Christians had caused them to feel this way. This experience was enlightening; it highlighted the gap between the church's intended witness and how some perceive it. It served as a powerful reminder for me to live out my faith authentically and to engage with others in a spirit of humility and love, striving to reflect the true character of Christ.

Personal Inventory:

How has God spoken to you through this chapter? What is God calling you to do about it?

Through this chapter (Chapter 4 – The Church), God has spoken to me about the importance of preserving and engaging with Church History, which is essential for our spiritual growth and understanding of the faith. I felt a strong conviction to shine a light in the darkness by advocating for a Church Library, as I believe it can serve as a valuable resource for our congregation. Recognizing the need for accessible materials on Church History and biblical teachings, I took the initiative to write a letter to our senior pastor, Dr. Ross Chandler, and Pastor Todd, recommending the establishment of a Church Library and/or a Digital Church Library to be integrated into our Mobile Application.

In response, I learned that the demand for a physical church library had dwindled, leading to its closure about three to four years ago. However, I was encouraged to hear that there is a possibility of creating a mini library in January 2025. Although space constraints in the church currently limit this initiative, I believe God is calling me to persist in advocating for this idea. This experience has deepened my understanding of the need for accessible resources that can help our congregation grow in knowledge and faith. I feel led to continue exploring creative solutions, perhaps by organizing book drives, collaborating with church members who may have resources to contribute, or even developing a digital resource hub that can be utilized in the meantime.

Ultimately, I am committed to following God's call by actively participating in the life of our church and ensuring that we have the tools necessary to educate and inspire our community. I trust that as I remain faithful in this endeavor, God will open doors for us to fulfill this vision.

14- MISSION APPLICATION PROJECT

Missions and Evangelism: Mission Application Project

Empowering Recovery and Evangelism: A Mission Application Project at The Mission Center (TMC) and Refuge Recovery Chuch (RRC)

I. Introduction and Overview of Topic (Mission Application Project also known as "MAP")

Over the past 8 weeks (Fall 2024), I have focused my Mission Application Project (MAP) on supporting the Refuge and Recovery Church (RRC) at The Mission Center (TMC) (408 Avenue R, Marble Falls, TX).[13] This church meets every Thursday from 6:00 to 8:00 pm CST, providing a safe and supportive environment for individuals in recovery from addiction. My mission work consisted of 7 hours of setting up, preparing music, and creating visual music slides using "ProPresenter" for RRC services. Additionally, I volunteered for 3 hours assisting with the TMC's phones and office tasks, helping Pastor Tucker Edwards, one of the staff pastors at First Baptist Church Marble Falls (FBCMF), and handing out Bibles around TMC.[14] This allowed Pastor Edwards to travel to Austin for a field survey and tour of Community First! Village (CFV), an initiative started by Mobile Loaves and Fishes (MLF).[15] By contributing to both the service and the operational support of TMC and RRC, I was able to play a small part in the ongoing work of ministry and outreach. This experience has deepened my understanding of how local churches can serve the needs of individuals facing addiction and homelessness while fostering community transformation. It has been a humbling opportunity to support these efforts and see firsthand the impact of faith-based outreach. The mission statement of RRC is based on Psalm 46:1, which highlights that God is our refuge and strength, offering help in times of trouble. This verse emphasizes the importance of relying on God for comfort, security,

---

[13] The Mission Center. "Home." *The Mission Center*. Accessed December 10, 2024. https://themissioncenter.com/.

[14] "Staff," First Baptist Church Marble Falls, accessed December 10, 2024, https://discoverfirst.com/about-us/staff/.

[15] Mobile Loaves & Fishes, "Community First! Village," accessed December 10, 2024, https://mlf.org/community-first/.

and empowerment, particularly during life's challenges. It affirms the belief that God equips us with the strength to overcome adversity, reinforcing the foundational truth of His constant presence and support.[16]

Moreover, I dedicated myself to fulfilling the goals of my Mission Application Project (MAP) by actively engaging in evangelistic efforts. I canvassed the Marble Falls area and nearby towns such as Kingsland, Burnet, and Granite Shoals, distributing Bibles to those I encountered. This outreach allowed me to initiate conversations about faith and offer spiritual encouragement to individuals in need. I approached people with the invitation to pray for them, often engaging in heartfelt prayers right there on the spot. For those who seemed hesitant or unsure, I quietly lifted them in prayer, interceding for their visible struggles and burdens.

Through these interactions, I witnessed moments of openness, gratitude, and transformation, which reinforced the power of personal connection in ministry. Each encounter deepened my understanding of the challenges many face and the profound impact of a simple act of kindness or a shared prayer. By offering spiritual support and tangible resources, I aimed to meet both the spiritual and practical needs of the community. These weeks have been a humbling reminder of the importance of stepping outside our comfort zones to bring Christ's love to others. This experience has strengthened my passion for evangelism and inspired me to continue serving and building relationships within the community. These weeks have been a humbling reminder of the importance of stepping outside our comfort zones to bring Christ's love to others. I am profoundly grateful for the opportunity to serve in this way, knowing that every interaction was a step toward planting seeds of hope and faith.

Missions and Suffering

In *Desiring God*, John Piper discusses the integral connection between missions and suffering, both of which play crucial roles in advancing God's kingdom. In Chapters 9 and 10, Piper emphasizes that the Christian life calls for active involvement in missions, particularly frontier missions where the gospel has yet to reach

---

[16] The Holy Bible: *English Standard Version*. Wheaton, IL: Crossway, 2001. (Psalm 46:1).

certain people groups. Chapter 9 urges believers to share the gospel with unreached communities, demonstrating the urgency of spreading God's message to every corner of the world. In Chapter 10, Piper shifts focus to suffering, asserting that Christians can find deep joy in suffering for Christ's mission. He references Paul's words in 2 Corinthians 11:24-29, where Paul describes the hardships he endures for the sake of the Church and Colossians 1:24, where Paul rejoices in his suffering because it serves to advance the church. This perspective aligns with my Mission Application Project (MAP) focused on evangelism and missions, where I am learning to serve others in their need, recognizing that reaching out through service, even at the cost of personal discomfort, honor God and further build His kingdom. Through this project, I am applying Piper's teachings by engaging in outreach efforts and understanding the deeper call of suffering in mission work.[17]

In Chapters 9 and 10 of *Desiring God*, John Piper emphasizes the critical importance of missions and the redemptive value of suffering in the Christian life. Piper's call to engage in frontier missions resonates with the biblical mandate to spread the gospel to all nations, as outlined in Matthew 28:19-20. He highlights the 10/40 window, a concept that identifies regions with the greatest need for evangelism and missionary efforts, underscoring the urgency of reaching unreached people groups. Piper's hero, Ralph Winter, a missionary theologian, is a source of inspiration, demonstrating how missions can radically transform lives and expand God's kingdom. In addition to missions, Piper discusses suffering for Christ, asserting that hardship, when endured for the gospel's sake, has redemptive value. This aligns with biblical teachings, such as 2 Corinthians 4:17, which highlights that present suffering is producing an eternal weight of glory far beyond comparison. Moreover, Paul's words in Colossians 1:24, where he rejoices in his sufferings for the church, reinforce the idea that suffering, when connected to God's mission, brings glory to Him and furthers His work in the world. Piper's theology challenges believers to not only embrace missions as central to the Christian life but also to view suffering as a means of participating in Christ's redemptive work, both of which contribute to the fulfillment of God's global purpose. Through these two aspects—missions and suffering—Piper helps

---

[17] John Piper, *Desiring God: Meditations of a Christian Hedonist* (Colorado Springs, CO: Multnomah Books, 2011), 224-225; The Holy Bible: *English Standard Version*. Wheaton, IL: Crossway, 2001. (2 Cor. 11:24-29, Col. 1:24).

believers understand how their lives, even in difficulty, can be a powerful testimony to God's glory and kingdom.[18]

II. Description of the Ministry Practice(s) Observed

During my Mission Application Project (MAP), I observed and participated in various ministry practices at The Mission Center (TMC) and Refuge and Recovery Church (RRC). A central focus was *evangelism*, as I handed out Bibles around TMC and engaged in meaningful conversations with individuals seeking spiritual encouragement. I also mentored men from His Joshua House (HJH) and women from Open Door Recovery House (ODRH), offering faith-based guidance and building trust through one-on-one conversations.[19] These interactions demonstrated the transformative power of personal engagement for those in recovery.

Discipleship was another key element, as RRC services utilized the *Recovery Bible* (New Living Translation, 2nd edition) to guide their spiritual growth. Testimonies and Bible teachings from speakers such as Business Owner David Clendennen, Pastor Tucker Edwards, Pastor George Perry, Chaplain Richard "Mark" Cartwright, Pastor David Henneke, Business Owner Allen Williams, and Joshua House Board Member Bob Clifton added depth and inspiration. Their shared experiences and biblical insights offered hope and encouragement to attendees.

Music and *worship* also played a significant role in the ministry. My wife contributed by singing during services, while I handled the music slides using "ProPresenter" and set up sound equipment to ensure a seamless worship experience. For example at RRC we sang songs like: "Here I Am To Worship" and "Goodness of God."[20] The

---

[18] John Piper, *Desiring God: Meditations of a Christian Hedonist* (Colorado Springs, CO: Multnomah Books, 2011), 230-252; Gailyn Van Rheenen, *Missions: Biblical Foundations and Contemporary Strategies*, 2nd ed. (Grand Rapids, MI: Zondervan, 2014), 458-459; The Holy Bible: *English Standard Version*. Wheaton, IL: Crossway, 2001. (Matt. 28:19-20, 2 Cor. 4:17, Col. 1:24); Ralph Winter, "When Jesus Said...," *Missions Frontiers* 17, no. 11-12 (Nov./Dec., 1995): 56.

[19] Open Door Recovery House, "*Home,*" accessed December 10, 2024, https://opendoorrecoveryhouse.org/; His Joshua House, "Home," accessed December 10, 2024, https://www.hisjoshuahouse.org/.

[20] Sean Shetler, "Here I Am to Worship," YouTube Channel, published September 13, 2024, https://www.youtube.com/shorts/WJsfUjpZYWU; Sean Shetler, "Goodness of God," YouTube Channel, published September 13, 2024,

integration of worship, testimonies, and teaching created a spiritually enriching atmosphere.

Every Thursday, *coffee* and *meals* were prepared and catered by Open Door Recovery House (ODRH), His Joshua House (HJH), or David and Myra Clendennen, lay leaders at First Baptist Church of Marble Falls (FBCMF) who oversee Refuge and Recovery Church (RRC) alongside members of these organizations which aided a sense of family, food, and *fellowship*. This collaboration fostered a supportive and inclusive environment for individuals recovering from addiction. Through these ministry practices, I witnessed how intentional acts of service, evangelism, and discipleship can create a transformative community that reflects God's love and grace. This experience deepened my appreciation for faith-based outreach addressing addiction and homelessness.

Lastly, *prayer* was a deeply emphasized practice at RRC. Following the third worship song, a collection plate was passed to support the ongoing operations of RRC, along with prayer cards for attendees to write down their prayer requests. One Thursday, Myra Clendennen shared a heartfelt reminder, encouraging everyone to utilize the prayer cards by saying, "If you write a prayer on that card, the women from Open Door Recovery House (ODRH) will pray over them—and you'll see how those prayers get answered."[21] This powerful testimony highlighted the significance of prayer in fostering faith and community within the ministry.

The Thief Comes to Steal, Kill, and Destroy

Engraved on the central support beam of our Church Sanctuary at FBCMF is John 10:10, which proclaims: *"The thief comes only to steal and kill and destroy. I came that they may have life and have it abundantly."*[22] This verse captures the essence of Jesus' purpose—offering life in its fullness, contrasting His mission with the

---

https://www.youtube.com/shorts/tcauDIWoWSI.

[21] Myra Clendennen, statement made during Refuge and Recovery Church service, The Mission Center, Marble Falls, TX, October 2024.

[22] John 10:10-11: uses the shepherd as a frequent metaphor for God's care of Israel (Ezek. 34:11-23; Isa. 40:11; Palm 23:1-4; Psalm 78:52-53; Psalm 95:7). See Michael D. Coogan, ed., *The New Oxford Annotated Bible with Apocrypha: New Revised Standard Version*, 5th ed. (Oxford: Oxford University Press, 2018), 1937.

destructive intentions of the thief (Satan). When a person struggles with addiction to alcohol or drugs, they are being robbed by Satan of their peace, joy, and potential. Addiction entangles individuals in a cycle of destruction, pulling them further away from the life God intended for them. In this battle, Satan seeks to steal their hope, while Jesus offers the freedom and healing that can restore them to wholeness. Addiction entangles individuals in a cycle of destruction, pulling them further away from the life God intended for them. In this battle, Satan seeks to steal their hope, while Jesus offers the freedom and healing that can restore them to wholeness. Through Christ's power, individuals can break free from the chains of addiction and embrace the abundant life He offers. As they surrender their struggles to Him, they begin to experience true restoration, gaining strength to rebuild their lives and fulfill God's purpose for them.

The Good Shepherd

The next, verse 11 introduces the metaphor of the *enigmatic* spiritual comparison of the Good Shepherd.[23] John uses the Greek term "παροιμία" (*paroimia*, Strong's #3942), which is translated as "metaphor," "figure of speech," or "proverb." This term also appears in John 10:6, where it refers to the metaphor Jesus had just shared in John 10:1-5, involving the shepherd, the sheep, and the gate. Scholars generally use these translations to convey that the term refers to a saying that is metaphorical, symbolic, or somewhat cryptic in nature. It indicates a form of speech not meant to be taken literally but instead designed to communicate deeper moral or spiritual truths through comparison or analogy. This teaching, rich in symbolic language, reveals Jesus' role as the Good Shepherd and the path of salvation, a concept His audience found difficult to understand. In Contrast, the *Synoptic Gospels*, where Jesus' teachings are often referred to using the Greek term "παραβολή" (*parabolē*, Strong's #3850) for parables, the Gospel of John does not use this term in his writing.[24]

---

[23] Merriam-Webster.com Dictionary, s.v. "enigmatic," accessed December 10, 2024, https://www.merriam-webster.com/dictionary/enigmatic.

[24] The Greek term "παροιμία" (*paroimia*, Strong's #3942), meaning "metaphor" or "figure of speech," is used five times in the New Testament, whereas the Greek term "παραβολή" (*parabolē*, Strong's #3850), meaning "parable," is used fifty times. The term "παροιμία" (*paroimia*) refers to a proverbial or metaphorical statement, and although John does not use the term for "parable" (παραβολή, *parabolē*), the verses

John does not use the term "παραβολή" (*parabolē*, Strong's #3850), which appears 50 times in the New Testament but is absent in the *Gospel of John*, instead employing terms such as "λόγος" (*logos*, Strong's #3056), meaning "word," "speech," or "reason" (used 330 times), and "παροιμία" (paroimia, Strong's #3942), meaning "metaphor" or "figure of speech" (used 5 times), as seen in John 10:6, where it refers to a metaphorical or proverbial statement. However, the verses in this discourse closely resemble the parables found in the Synoptic tradition, blending metaphorical imagery with profound spiritual truths.[25]

Heart of Addiction

In *The Heart of Addiction: A Biblical Perspective*, Dr. Mark Shaw, theologian, author, and founder of Truth in Love Ministries, discusses the transformative process for addicts in Chapter 4, "Who Are You?" He explains that after counseling over a thousand addicts, he has derived observations that will aid in the process of change. Shaw distinguishes between "biblically-derived" principles, which are implied but not explicitly stated in Scripture, and "biblically-directed" principles, which are direct commands from the Bible. He notes that some observations and metaphors in the chapter may not be biblically based.[26]

---

in the Gospel of John closely resemble the parables found in the Synoptic Gospels; "Synoptic Gospels," *Encyclopedia Britannica*, June 5, 2024, https://www.britannica.com/topic/Synoptic-Gospels. See William D. Mounce, *Mounce's Complete Expository Dictionary of Old and New Testament Words* (Grand Rapids, MI: Zondervan, 2006), 1232-1237; The Holy Bible: *English Standard Version*. Wheaton, IL: Crossway, 2001. (John 10:1-11).

[25] John does not use the term "παραβολή" (parabolē, Strong's #3850), which appears 50 times in the New Testament but is absent in John, instead employing terms such as "λόγος" (logos, Strong's #3056), meaning "word," "speech," or "reason" (used 330 times), and "παροιμία" (paroimia, Strong's #3942), meaning "metaphor" or "figure of speech" (used 5 times), as seen in John 10:6, where it refers to a metaphorical or proverbial statement. See William D. Mounce, *Mounce's Complete Expository Dictionary of Old and New Testament Words* (Grand Rapids, MI: Zondervan, 2006), 1202-1237.

[26] Mark E. Shaw, *The Heart of Addiction: A Biblical Perspective* (Bemidji, MN: Focus Publishing, 2008), 30-31.

God Ponders the Heart

Dr. Shaw encourages us to examine our hearts, particularly in relation to substance abuse and addiction. He highlights that only God truly knows what is within a person's heart, as Jeremiah 17:9-10 reveals: "The heart is deceitful above all things, and desperately sick; who can understand it? I the Lord search the heart and test the mind, to give every man according to his ways, according to the fruit of his deeds." Shaw emphasizes that we cannot always know our own hearts, and secular teachings that claim truth comes from within are misguided.[27]

Everything Flows From the Heart

Proverbs 4:23 warns, "Keep your heart with all vigilance, for from it flow the springs of life," underlining the importance of guarding our hearts. Since all humans are born into sin (Romans 3:23), self-examination is often flawed without the guidance of God's Word and community. Without the illuminating guidance of God's Word and the support of a trusted community, we can easily misinterpret our motivations and actions. Thus, seeking God's wisdom and accountability is essential to ensure that our hearts align with His will. As we navigate life, our hearts are influenced by both internal and external forces, often pulling us away from God's truth. To effectively guard our hearts, we must intentionally align our desires with His Word, seeking continual transformation through the Holy Spirit. By doing so, we protect ourselves from negative influences and cultivate a heart that mirrors God's love and righteousness in every part of our lives. As we constantly renew our minds through Scripture and rely on the Holy Spirit's power, we develop a heart that stands firm in faith, becoming more resilient in the face of life's trials. This ongoing process allows us to reflect God's transforming grace in our daily actions and relationships. Additionally, there is power in community and fellowship with other believers. 1 Peter 5:8

---

[27] The Holy Bible: *English Standard Version*. Wheaton, IL: Crossway, 2001. (Jer. 17:9-10); Mark E. Shaw, *The Heart of Addiction: A Biblical Perspective* (Bemidji, MN: Focus Publishing, 2008), 30-31.

states: "Be sober-minded, be watchful. Your adversary the devil prowls around like a roaring lion, seeking someone to devour."[28]

Man is Blind and Needs the Truth

Man is blind and needs the truth of God found outside the heart of man – in the pages of the Bible – in order to illuminate his heart and motives. Man needs to put God's truth within his heart by studying, memorizing, and meditating upon the Holy Scriptures (Psalm 1:1).[29] To examine the motives and desires of his heart, the addict must believe the truth found in Hebrews 4:12-13: "For the word of God is living and active, sharper than any two-edged sword, piercing to the division of soul and of spirit, of joints and of marrow, and discerning the thoughts and intentions of the heart. And no creature is hidden from his sight, but all are naked and exposed to the eyes of him to whom we must give account." This passage emphasizes the power and penetrating ability of God's Word to reveal the deepest aspects of the human heart and hold all accountable before God.[30]

We Take Every Thought Captive to Obey Christ

In 2 Corinthians 10:5, Paul emphasizes the crucial task of controlling our thoughts, ensuring they align with God's truth and rejecting anything that opposes His will. This verse highlights the active responsibility believers have in guarding their minds and making every thought obedient to Christ. Paul states, "We destroy arguments and every lofty opinion raised against the knowledge of God, and take every thought captive to obey Christ."[31] Paul encourages believers to confront and dismantle any arguments or ideas that oppose the knowledge of God, reinforcing the need for a focused commitment to spiritual obedience (Romans 12:2; Philippians 4:8). This command underscores the transformative

---

[28] The Holy Bible: *English Standard Version*. Wheaton, IL: Crossway, 2001. (Prov. 4:23, Rom. 3:23, 1 Pet. 5:8); Mark E. Shaw, *The Heart of Addiction: A Biblical Perspective* (Bemidji, MN: Focus Publishing, 2008), 31-32.

[29] Ibid., (Psalm 1:1).

[30] Ibid., (Heb. 4:12-13).

[31] Ibid., (2 Cor. 10:5).

power of aligning our thoughts with God's Word and maintaining a disciplined mind in the pursuit of holiness.[32]

III. Critical Analysis and Evaluation

Theophanies—divine manifestations in tangible forms—are closely tied to the spiritual mission work carried out by organizations such as TMC (The Mission Center), RRC (Restoration Recovery Center), and First Baptist Church of Marble Falls (FBCMF).[33] These ministries embody the enactment of God's will through personal encounters and divine guidance. *Theophanies* like the Burning Bush (Exodus 3:2-6), the Pillar of Fire and Cloud (Exodus 13:21-22, Exodus 40:34-38), and the Angel of the Lord (Genesis 16:7-13, Judges 6:11-24) provide insights into how God reveals His presence and directs His people in both extraordinary and everyday contexts.[34]

The Burning Bush: Divine Calling and Purpose

In the account of the Burning Bush (Exodus 3:2-6), Moses encounters a bush that burns without being consumed, symbolizing a divine calling and the holiness of God. Moses' mission to lead the Israelites out of Egypt parallels the work of ministries like TMC and RRC, where individuals are called to serve those in need, manifesting God's presence through acts of compassion. At TMC, volunteers are called to help the homeless, veterans, addicts, and refugees, mirroring Moses' response to God's calling to a higher purpose. This divine calling is similar to the prayers spoken over individuals in ministries like the Open Door Recovery House (ODRH) group, where Myra Clendennen noted the powerful impact of prayer on the lives of those in recovery (Psalm 56:8). Thus, the Burning Bush theophany highlights how God's will is revealed

---

[32] The Holy Bible: *English Standard Version*. Wheaton, IL: Crossway, 2001. (Rom 12:2, Phil 4:8).

[33] "Theophany." *Encyclopedia Britannica*, January 23, 2024. https://www.britannica.com/topic/theophany.

[34] The Holy Bible: *English Standard Version*. Wheaton, IL: Crossway, 2001. (Gen 16:7-13, Ex. 3:2-40:38, Judges 6:11-24).

through purposeful actions and faithful prayer, guiding the volunteers at TMC and RRC to serve with divine intention.[35]

The Pillar of Fire and Cloud: Divine Guidance

The Pillar of Fire and Cloud (Exodus 13:21-22) provided the Israelites with divine guidance during their wilderness journey. This theophany illustrates God's continued presence and direction in the lives of His people. Similarly, the members of RRC and FBCMF receive guidance in their ministries, often in the form of synchronicities and divine inspiration that direct their efforts in helping individuals battling addiction, homelessness, and spiritual struggles. Just as God's pillar gave the Israelites clear direction, ministries like RRC experience God's tangible guidance, often in the form of transformative moments and revelations that align with His greater purpose.[36]

Psalm 56:8 encapsulates this divine intimacy, where God sees every tear, just as the ministries at RRC and TMC reflect God's intimate involvement in the lives of those they serve. God's presence, symbolized by the cloud or fire, serves as a sign of direction, just as it is experienced by the ministries as they fulfill their mission with divine timing and clarity.[37]

The Angel of the Lord: Personal Encounter and Divine Intervention

The Angel of the Lord (Genesis 16:7-13; Judges 6:11-24) serves as a personal messenger, intervening in the lives of individuals to guide them in God's will. These encounters often lead to a message of hope, redemption, or a call to action. For example, when the Angel of the Lord appeared to Gideon, it marked the beginning of his mission to lead Israel against the Midianites, despite his initial doubts. In similar ways, TMC, RRC, and FBCMF facilitate personal

---

[35] The Holy Bible: *English Standard Version*. Wheaton, IL: Crossway, 2001. (Ex. 3:2-6, Psalm 56:8).

[36] The Holy Bible: *English Standard Version*. Wheaton, IL: Crossway, 2001. (Ex. 13:21-22).

[37] The Holy Bible: *English Standard Version*. Wheaton, IL: Crossway, 2001. (Psalm 56:8).

encounters with God's calling through prayer, counsel, and emotional support to those in crisis. These encounters, parallel to those experienced by biblical figures, reveal divine wisdom and clarity, guiding individuals in fulfilling their service.[38]

Synchronicities and Divine Wisdom

Divine wisdom and synchronicity—where God's will aligns with the timing of life's events—play a significant role in ministries like TMC, RRC, and FBCMF. In Acts 2:17, the Holy Spirit is poured out, and people experience visions and dreams as forms of divine revelation. These synchronicities are evident when individuals find themselves in the right place at the right time, reflecting the active presence of God in their lives. Dr. Jenee Walker once said, "Even now, there are no coincidences, only divine appointments."[39] Stories from these ministries, where individuals walk into the center at a pivotal moment, demonstrate how God's plan unfolds through serendipitous events. Romans 8:28 further reinforce this idea by assuring believers that "All things work together for good for those who are called according to His purpose." This verse aligns with the belief that every effort in these ministries is guided by a higher purpose, often revealed through these seemingly coincidental but powerful moments.[40]

Some Key Lessons Learned

One of the keynote speakers, Chaplain Richard "Mark" Cartwright, shared his personal testimony, reflecting on the biblical passage where Jesus instructs those around Him to help Lazarus come out of the tomb. Lazarus, still wrapped in burial cloths, is told by Jesus, "Unbind him, and let him go" (John 11:44). This act of removing Lazarus' grave clothes carries deep symbolism. First, it highlights the completeness of Lazarus' resurrection—he was not

---

[38] The Holy Bible: *English Standard Version*. Wheaton, IL: Crossway, 2001. (Gen. 16:7-13, Jud. 6:11-14).

[39] Jenee Walker, "Even Now: There Are No Coincidences, Only Divine Appointments," *Dr. Jenee Walker*, June 29, 2020, https://www.drrjeneewalker.com/single-post/2020/06/29/-even-now-there-are-no-coincidences-only-divine-appointments.

[40] The Holy Bible: *English Standard Version*. Wheaton, IL: Crossway, 2001. (Acts 2:17, Rom. 8:28).

merely revived but fully restored, showcasing Christ's power over life and death. This moment also serves as a metaphor for the spiritual transformation available to believers, where they shed the "grave clothes" of sin and embrace a new identity in Christ (Romans 6:4, Ephesians 4:22-24). The call to remove the "old self" and live a righteous life is a common theme throughout Scripture, particularly in passages like Ephesians 4:22 and Colossians 3:9-10. Chaplain Cartwright connected this to the importance of releasing the past, saying, "Don't carry the baggage. You need to let go of what Jesus set you free from... Let the trauma go away. God set you free and you need to take off your grave clothes."[41]

John 8:36 states, *"So if the Son sets you free, you will be free indeed."* This verse highlights the deep, spiritual freedom that is granted through Christ. It affirms that true liberation is found only through Him, emphasizing the transformative power of His freedom. Jesus' statement connects to His role as the source of true freedom, which is both spiritual and eternal (John 8:31-32; Galatians 5:1). According to theologians, this freedom transcends earthly limitations, offering believers freedom from the bondage of sin and death. Scholars also point out that in John's gospel; freedom is intricately tied to knowing the truth, which is embodied in Christ Himself (John 14:6).[42]

Additionally, Chaplain Cartwright shared insights from Ephesians 4:11-12, discussing the fivefold ministries of the Church. He reflected on his personal challenges, including facing adversity after his divorce, which initially hindered his ability to find traditional ministry roles. However, by surrendering and trusting in God's plan, he now serves as a chaplain with the Texas Department of Criminal Justice (TDCJ), working in a women's prison. This story highlights the transformative power of embracing God's calling, even in the face of personal struggles and non-traditional paths.[43]

---

[41] Richard "Mark" Cartwright, quote from his testimony on John 11:44, October 2024; The Holy Bible: *English Standard Version*. Wheaton, IL: Crossway, 2001. (John 11:44, Rom. 6:4, Eph. 4:22-24, Col. 3:9-10).

[42] The Holy Bible: *English Standard Version*. Wheaton, IL: Crossway, 2001. (John 8:31-36, Gal. 5:1, John 14:6).

[43] The Holy Bible: *English Standard Version*. Wheaton, IL: Crossway, 2001. (Eph. 4:11-12).

The Paradox of Powerlessness

Another speaker, Bob Clifton, who has been sober for over 30 years and serves as a board member of the HJH, shared his insights during his talk. He discussed Step 1 of the recovery process, which emphasizes the recognition that we are powerless over our addictions and need God's help. This aligns with the concept of Divine Providence, which underscores that God is the one who saves the sinner, while we still have the free will to choose to come to Him. Romans 10:13 states, *"For everyone who calls on the name of the Lord will be saved,"* which highlights the universal availability of God's grace, and ties in with themes found in other passages such as Joel 2:32, Romans 7:24, and John 15:5.[44]

The concept of powerlessness is central in addiction recovery, particularly in recovery-focused resources like the *Recovery Study Bible and 2 Corinthians 4:7-10*.[45] This concept highlights that individuals cannot manage their addiction through their own strength or willpower. The "powerless paradox" reflects the idea that admitting powerlessness is not a sign of weakness, but rather a step towards empowerment. By acknowledging their inability to control their addiction, individuals open themselves up to receiving strength from a higher power—God. This paradox emphasizes that through surrendering control, individuals gain access to divine support, enabling them to change their lives.

In 2 Corinthians 4:7-10 (NLT), Paul speaks about the paradox of powerlessness, highlighting that though we may face trials and afflictions, we are not defeated because of the strength God provides. This passage relates closely to Step 1 in the recovery process, where individuals acknowledge their powerlessness over addiction and their need for divine help. The paradox is that by admitting our weakness, we open ourselves to God's power, enabling us to endure and overcome. This concept of powerlessness is often seen as a necessary step for empowerment, as recovery begins with surrendering control to a higher power. Paul writes, "We now have this light shining in our hearts, but we ourselves are like fragile clay

---

[44] The Holy Bible: English Standard Version. Wheaton, IL: Crossway, 2001. (Rom. 10:13, Joel 2:32, Rom. 7:24, John 15:5).

[45] *The Recovery Study Bible: New Living Translation*, 2nd ed. (Carol Stream, IL: Tyndale House Publishers, 2011), 1483, (2 Cor. 4:7-10).

jars containing this great treasure. This makes it clear that our great power is from God, not from ourselves" (2 Corinthians 4:7 NLT). This aligns with the principle of accepting one's limitations to gain strength from God, a core aspect of many recovery programs.

The *Recovery Study Bible* (Pg. 1483) further elaborates on the paradox of powerlessness in recovery.[46] The idea is that recognizing one's inability to control life through sheer willpower opens the door for God to work through us. In addiction recovery, as in life's struggles, powerlessness is not a defeat but a gateway to spiritual transformation, where believers rely on God's strength to overcome the darkness in their lives. This powerful insight into human weakness and divine strength can be empowering for those in recovery, as it reflects the deep spiritual truth that surrendering to God leads to true freedom and healing. This principle is not about passivity but about regaining control in a healthier, more sustainable way. By surrendering personal control to God, individuals can navigate their struggles and transform unmanageable behaviors. This principle extends beyond addiction and can apply to any area of life where control has become overwhelming, such as unhealthy relationships, work-a-holism, or chronic stress. Ultimately, it encourages individuals to recognize areas where they are powerless and surrender them to God's will for a more balanced and fulfilling life.

Doing God's Will

The work carried out by TMC, RRC, and FBCMF exemplifies the way God's will is revealed through theophanies. Just as Moses experienced God's call through the Burning Bush, and the Israelites were guided by the Pillar of Fire and Cloud, the leaders and volunteers in these ministries respond to God's calling to serve others. These theophanies reveal a profound spiritual truth: that God's will is active, accessible, and tangible in the lives of His followers. Through prayer, synchronicities, dreams, and personal encounters, God's wisdom and guidance continue to manifest, ensuring His purpose is fulfilled in the lives of those serving others. These ministries illustrate how God's presence is not only revealed in miraculous events but also in the everyday acts of love, service,

---

[46] Step 1. Paradox of Powerlessness in Recovery. *The Recovery Study Bible: New Living Translation*, 2nd ed. (Carol Stream, IL: Tyndale House Publishers, 2011), 1483. (2 Cor. 4:7-10).

and restoration, making His will evident in both extraordinary and mundane moments of life.

Moreover, these ministries highlight the relational nature of God's will, where His presence is found not only in grand miracles but in the simplicity of caring for the brokenhearted and the marginalized. This dynamic interplay of divine calling and human response creates a living testimony of faith. In doing so, they show how God's purposes are accomplished through both spiritual encounters and practical service. Such work invites all believers to recognize and participate in God's ongoing redemptive plan in the world.

In addition to the practical and spiritual work of these ministries, their mission reflects the biblical mandate to care for those in need. James 1:27 reminds us, *"Religion that is pure and undefiled before God, the Father, is this: to visit orphans and widows in their affliction, and to keep oneself unstained from the world."*[47] This verse highlights the essence of God's will as one rooted in compassionate action and moral integrity. Through their efforts to aid the homeless, addicted, and marginalized, TMC, RRC, and FBCMF embody this scriptural call to serve others selflessly. By stepping into the lives of those facing hardship, they act as tangible extensions of God's love and provision. Such service not only fulfills a divine commission but also nurtures deeper spiritual growth and community transformation, demonstrating how God's Word inspires and sustains holistic ministry efforts. This work serves as a powerful reminder that obedience to God's will not only transforms the lives of those being served but also enriches the faith and purpose of those who serve, creating a cycle of grace and renewal within the community.

IV. Conclusion Key Reflections and Observations

The Mission Application Project (MAP) that I participated in over the past 8 weeks has provided significant insights into the vital role faith-based initiatives play in addressing addiction, evangelism, and homelessness. Specifically, my work with Refuge and Recovery Church (RRC) and The Mission Center (TMC) has revealed the profound impact that local churches can have in meeting both spiritual and physical needs within the community. Through my various responsibilities—ranging from helping with music

---

[47] The Holy Bible: *English Standard Version*. Wheaton, IL: Crossway, 2001. (James 1:27).

preparation and technical tasks to supporting Pastor Tucker Edwards with operational duties and outreach—I gained a deeper understanding of how churches and ministries can integrate their faith into tangible outreach efforts, providing both emotional and practical support to individuals in recovery and experiencing homelessness.

A key observation throughout this project was the importance of creating a safe and supportive environment for those recovering from addiction and homelessness. The church services at RRC are not just opportunities for worship but serve as a vital refuge where individuals can share their experiences, find healing, and receive the encouragement they need to continue their recovery journey. According to one study, faith-based recovery programs are effective because they address both the spiritual and emotional dimensions of recovery, enabling individuals to experience profound transformations.[48] This aligns with the mission of RRC, grounded in Psalm 46:1, which emphasizes God's role as a source of refuge and strength in times of trouble. The inclusion of this verse in the church's mission statement underpins the spiritual foundation that guides the church's outreach efforts, focusing on God's ability to empower individuals during their recovery process.

Moreover, my involvement in preparing visual music slides and setting up for services was an integral part of creating a worship environment that facilitated spiritual engagement. Music and worship serve as tools that connect individuals to God's presence, fostering emotional healing and spiritual renewal. In a report by Thomas (2020), the role of music in recovery programs is highlighted as a means of reducing anxiety and creating a sense of belonging and comfort. By ensuring the visual aspects of the service were aligned with the music, I contributed to the overall experience, helping attendees to focus their attention on the message of hope and restoration.[49]

In addition to my work with RRC, volunteering for office tasks at TMC exposed me to the broader operational aspects of ministry and

---

[48] Gall, T. L. (2017). "The Role of Faith-Based Programs in Recovery from Addiction." *Journal of Substance Abuse Treatment*, 72, 34-42.

[49] R. P. Thomas, "The Role of Music in Addiction Recovery Programs," *Journal of Addiction Research & Therapy* 8, no. 2 (2020): 65–74.

outreach. My time spent assisting with phone calls and distributing Bibles allowed me to witness firsthand the church's commitment to providing practical support to those in need. This operational involvement also allowed Pastor Edwards to travel to Austin for a field survey of Community First! Village (CFV), a ministry focused on providing affordable housing and support to the homeless. The partnership between TMC and CFV demonstrates how churches can actively engage with community initiatives that address homelessness, showing that outreach efforts can extend beyond immediate spiritual care into long-term solutions for people in need.

A significant takeaway from this experience was the interconnectedness of spiritual and practical outreach. The work of RRC and TMC serves as a model for how churches can build holistic programs that address not only the emotional and spiritual needs of individuals but also their physical and social needs. As Wright (2019) explains, faith-based initiatives that combine both spiritual and practical support are often more successful in promoting long-term recovery, as they empower individuals to find healing on multiple levels. This dual focus reflects the Christian calling to love and serve others, especially those on the margins of society.[50]

Duplicity, Deceitfulness, and Darkness: A Reflection on the Fragmented Will

When the human will is detached from God, it becomes marked by duplicity—more accurately described as fragmentation and multiplicity. The will is drawn to many conflicting desires, which cannot coexist in harmony. Without God, the mind and emotions descend into disorder, leading to internal conflict. While this turmoil may not be immediately acknowledged, the will can appear deceptively simple at first glance. For example, deciding to go to the store for milk and bread, or choosing whether to tell the truth, seems straightforward, almost effortless. These decisions seem as uncomplicated as a light breeze. However, this apparent simplicity masks the complexity of the will's actions, which are invisible and non-physical in nature. As W.B. Yeats poetically asked, "Who can distinguish darkness from the soul?" The inner workings of the will are not as immediately apparent as tangible objects like a lamp or pen. On deeper reflection, one realizes that an act of the will is far from simple. It involves a complex web of thoughts, feelings,

---

[50] N. T. Wright, *Faith and Works: Serving God Through Holistic Ministry* (Grand Rapids: Zondervan, 2019), 45-49.

purposes, and motivations, each influencing the nature and strength of the decision. The interweaving of these factors demonstrates that what appears to be a simple choice is, in reality, an intricate process affected by many underlying actions and desires. This reflects the spiritual tension within a will that is disconnected from God, where inner fragmentation prevents the person from functioning in a unified way. True clarity and unity are only achieved when the will is aligned with God's will, allowing for decisions that reflect His guidance. Without such alignment, the will remains trapped in confusion and disorder, distorting choices and preventing the individual from moving forward with divine purpose.[51]

People Who Are Redeemed For Redemptive Living

In *The Mission of God's People*, Wright discusses the Exodus as a foundational event in understanding God's redemptive work. He emphasizes that God's act of deliverance in the Exodus was comprehensive, addressing not only Israel's physical, political, and social oppression but also establishing a new relationship between Israel and the living God. This transformative act was not merely about freeing Israel from slavery; it was about bringing them into a new identity and a covenantal relationship with God. Wright argues that the Exodus event is a prime example of how God works in history with purpose, motivated by His own desire to define His character and identity.[52]

This redemptive act was a total response to Israel's total need, encompassing both their immediate historical circumstances and their spiritual journey. By acting in history, God revealed His character and established a permanent definition of His identity through the name YHWH, which became intimately connected to His people and His actions. Wright points out that the Exodus narrative serves as a definitive case study of God's overarching mission and the way He engages with the world to bring about redemption, both in a physical and spiritual sense.[53]

---

[51] Dallas Willard, *Renovation of the Heart: Putting on the Character of Christ* (Colorado Springs, CO: NavPress, 2012), 147.

[52] Christopher J. H. Wright, *The Mission of God's People: A Biblical Theology of the Church's Mission*, ed. Jonathan Lunde (Grand Rapids, MI: Zondervan, 2010), 271-273.

[53] Ibid., 270-272.

In essence, the Exodus was not just an event of historical significance, but a paradigm of God's ongoing mission to rescue, redeem, and transform His people in both their material and spiritual conditions. This foundational event continues to shape the understanding of how God's mission works in the world today, particularly in the way that God's mission intersects with human history and the deep, transformative need of His people (Wright, *The Mission of God's People*, 2010).[54]

This insight into God's total engagement with Israel's needs can be applied to the mission work at TMC and RRC, as they reflect the same holistic approach to serving those in need—both spiritually and practically. The mission of RRC, which is grounded in Psalm 46:1, follows this pattern by addressing not just the spiritual aspects of recovery, but also the emotional, social, and physical aspects of those recovering from addiction.[55] This holistic approach mirrors Christ's ministry, where He not only preached the gospel but also healed the sick, provided for the poor, and met the physical needs of the people (Matthew 4:24).[56] Similarly, TMC and RRC strive to embody Christ's love by offering a comprehensive support system, integrating spiritual guidance with practical resources for those in need, demonstrating that the Kingdom of God is both a present and future reality in the lives of believers.

Closing Thoughts

However, while this mission experience provided valuable insights into the work of local churches in addiction, evangelism, and homelessness outreach, it also highlighted some challenges. One such challenge is the need for more resources and trained volunteers to sustain these initiatives long term. As I assisted with office tasks and saw the impact of outreach efforts, it became clear that many of these ministries rely heavily on volunteers and donations. Expanding their impact would require consistent support and resources from the wider church community.

---

[54] Christopher J. H. Wright, *The Mission of God's People: A Biblical Theology of the Church's Mission*, ed. Jonathan Lunde (Grand Rapids, MI: Zondervan, 2010), 271-274.

[55] The Holy Bible: *English Standard Version*. Wheaton, IL: Crossway, 2001. (Psalm 46:1).

[56] Ibid., (Matt. 4:24).

14- MISSION APPLICATION PROJECT

Furthermore, my involvement in the Mission Application Project (MAP) with RRC and TMC has profoundly deepened my understanding of how local churches can actively address societal issues like addiction and homelessness. Additionally, I saw that the Church as whole does not have much training and equipping its members for evangelism and local missions. This experience has highlighted that faith-based initiatives go beyond spiritual renewal—they also address the practical needs of individuals in recovery and discipleship. By combining spiritual care with operational support, churches can create holistic solutions that empower individuals to overcome addiction and rebuild their lives. As I move forward, I am eager to continue supporting such initiatives, which serve as tangible expressions of God's love and transformative power for those in need. Moreover, the Church can foster its growth and sustainability in local missions and evangelism by equipping its members with the necessary tools and spiritual guidance. Garry Friesen, in *Decision Making and the Will of God*, highlights the role of spiritual gifts in this process. He explains, "The believer's spiritual gift is part of his or her ability and aptitude and so influences his or her decision making." Friesen emphasizes the Apostle Paul's teaching in 1 Corinthians 12:4-7, describing spiritual gifts as "gifts," "ministries," "effects," and "manifestations of the Spirit," granted for the common good. These gifts, divinely given, enable believers to engage in effective ministry. Furthermore, 1 Peter 4:10 underscores this responsibility: "As each one has received a special gift, employ it in serving one another as good stewards of the manifold grace of God." By recognizing and cultivating these gifts, the Church can empower its members to contribute meaningfully to its mission, fulfilling the moral will of God and advancing His kingdom.[57]

---

[57] Garry Friesen with J. Robin Maxson, *Decision Making and the Will of God*, 25th Anniversary Ed., Revised and Updated (New York: Multnomah Publishers, 2004), 345; The Holy Bible: *English Standard Version*. Wheaton, IL: Crossway, 2001. (1 Cor. 12:4-7, 1 Peter 4:10).

Closing Thoughts

In his book *Missions: Biblical Foundations and Contemporary Strategies*, Gailyn Van Rheenan emphasizes the significant impact of short-term missions on church members, noting how these experiences often ignite a deeper passion for the long-term mission of the church.

He cites Scott Moreau, who aptly states, "There simply is no substitute for hands-on ministry when the goal is creating hearts burdened for the task." This idea resonates with my own experiences at RRC and TMC, where direct involvement in serving others has deepened my commitment to the mission and created a stronger burden for the individuals we serve. Engaging in hands-on ministry has provided me with tangible insights into the real needs of the community, enhancing my understanding of the challenges faced by those we assist. Through these experiences, I have seen how short-term missions can transform individual hearts, empowering believers to respond more effectively to God's call for long-term service. Moreover, this active participation has allowed me to witness the profound impact of evangelism and service on both the individuals we serve and the volunteers involved. This deeper connection has strengthened my conviction that active participation in ministry is essential for fostering a lasting and meaningful commitment to God's mission.[58]

---

[58] Gailyn Van Rheenan, *Missions: Biblical Foundations and Contemporary Strategies* (Grand Rapids, MI: Zondervan, 2014), 436-437.

BIBLIOGRAPHY

Breen, Mike, and Steve Cockram. *Building a Discipling Culture.* Pauley's Island, SC: 3DM, 2009; revised 2011.

Cartwright, Richard "Mark." *Quote from his testimony on John 11:44,* October 2024.

Clendennen, Myra. *Statement made during Refuge and Recovery Church service,* The Mission Center, Marble Falls, TX, October 2024.

Coogan, Michael D., ed. *The New Oxford Annotated Bible with Apocrypha: New Revised Standard Version.* 5th ed. New York: Oxford University Press, 2018.

Encyclopedia Britannica. "*Theophany.*" Last modified January 23, 2024. https://www.britannica.com/topic/theophany.

———. "*Synoptic Gospels.*" June 5, 2024. https://www.britannica.com/topic/Synoptic-Gospels.

Foster, Richard J. *Celebration of Discipline: The Path to Spiritual Growth.* Special Anniversary Edition. San Francisco: HarperOne, 2018.

Friesen, Garry, with J. Robin Maxson. *Decision Making and the Will of God.* 25th Anniversary Ed., Revised and Updated. New York: Multnomah Publishers, 2004.

Gall, T. L. "*The Role of Faith-Based Programs in Recovery from Addiction.*" Journal of Substance Abuse Treatment 72 (2017): 34-42.

Hamilton, Mark, ed. *Transforming Word: One-Volume Commentary on the Bible.* Abilene, TX: Abilene Christian University Press, 2009.

Hillerbrand, H. J., and Matt Stefon. "*Christology.*" Encyclopedia Britannica. July 30, 2022. https://www.britannica.com/topic/Christology.

His Joshua House. "*Home.*" Accessed December 10, 2024. https://www.hisjoshuahouse.org/.

Keller, Tim. "*Basis of Prayer: 'Our Father.'*" Sermon, April 23, 1995. http://sermons2.redeemer.com/sermons/basis-prayer-our-father (accessed November 13, 2024).

Merriam-Webster.com Dictionary. "*Enigmatic.*" Accessed December 10, 2024. https://www.merriam-webster.com/dictionary/enigmatic.

_____. s.v. "*Triplet.*" Accessed December 9, 2024. https://www.merriam-webster.com/dictionary/triplet.

Mobile Loaves & Fishes. "*Community First! Village.*" Accessed December 10, 2024. https://mlf.org/community-first/.

Mounce, William D. *Mounce's Complete Expository Dictionary of Old and New Testament Words.* Grand Rapids, MI: Zondervan, 2006.

Murray, Andrew. *Humility: Essential Christian Classics.* CreateSpace Independent Publishing Platform, November 2, 2014.

Open Door Recovery House. "*Home.*" Accessed December 10, 2024. https://opendoorrecoveryhouse.org/.

Piper, John. *Desiring God: Meditations of a Christian Hedonist.* Colorado Springs, CO: Multnomah Books, 2011.

Rheenan, Gailyn Van. *Missions: Biblical Foundations and Contemporary Strategies.* Grand Rapids: Zondervan, 2014.

Schuller, Robert H. *Tough Times Never Last, But Tough People Do!.* Nashville, TN: Thomas Nelson, 1983.

Shetler, Sean. "*Goodness of God.*" YouTube Channel, published September 13, 2024. https://www.youtube.com/shorts/tcauDIWoWSI.

_____. "*Here I Am to Worship.*" YouTube Channel, published September 13, 2024. https://www.youtube.com/shorts/WJsfUjpZYWU.

"Staff." *First Baptist Church Marble Falls*. Accessed December 10, 2024. https://discoverfirst.com/about-us/staff/.

The Holy Bible: *English Standard Version*. Wheaton, IL: Crossway, 2001.

The Mission Center. "*Home*." The Mission Center. Accessed December 10, 2024. https://themissioncenter.com/.

The Recovery Study Bible: *New Living Translation*. 2nd ed. Carol Stream, IL: Tyndale House Publishers, 2011.

Thomas, R. P. "*The Role of Music in Addiction Recovery Programs*." *Journal of Addiction Research & Therapy* 8, no. 2 (2020): 65–74.

Van Rheenan, Gailyn. *Missions: Biblical Foundations and Contemporary Strategies*. Grand Rapids, MI: Zondervan, 2014.

Walker, Jenee. "*Even Now: There Are No Coincidences, Only Divine Appointments*." *Dr. Jenee Walker*, June 29, 2020. https://www.drrjeneewalker.com/single-post/2020/06/29/-even-now-there-are-no-coincidences-only-divine-appointments.

Willard, Dallas. *Renovation of the Heart: Putting on the Character of Christ*. Colorado Springs, CO: NavPress, 2012.

Winter, Ralph. "*When Jesus Said…*," *Missions Frontiers* 17, no. 11-12 (Nov./Dec., 1995): 56.

Wright, Christopher J. H. *The Mission of God's People: A Biblical Theology of the Church's Mission*. Edited by Jonathan Lunde. Grand Rapids, MI: Zondervan, 2010.

Wright, N. T. *Faith and Works: Serving God Through Holistic Ministry*. Grand Rapids: Zondervan, 2019.

Printed in Great Britain
by Amazon